THE CONTEMPORARY CONDITION

LOS ANGELES ARCHITECTURE

JAMES STEELE

To Carole
Dave

THE CONTEMPORARY CONDITION

LOS ANGELES ARCHITECTURE

JAMES STEELE

Φ

For Charles Moore

Phaidon Press Limited
Regent's Wharf
All Saints Street
London N1 9PA

First published 1993
First paperback edition 1998

© 1993 Phaidon Press
Limited

ISBN 0 7148 2869 6
(hardback)
ISBN 0 7148 3756 3
(paperback)

A CIP catalogue record for this
book is available from the
British Library.

Printed in Hong Kong

Acknowledgements
The author would particularly like to recognize the help of Kimberly
Kirkpatrick, who assisted in the initial research phase of this
project and in the compiling of the text, as well as Kelly Mullens
for the final information gathering, and my son Christopher, who
contributed several key ideas and sources to it. Thanks also, in
alphabetical order, to Francis Anderton, Lyn Blieler, Katherine
Coleman, Frank Dimster, John Enright, Douglas Gardner, Frank
Gehry, Robert Harris, Frank Israel, Pierre Koenig, Ralph Knowles,
Panos Koulermos, Charles Lagreco, Thom Mayne, Mary Eaves
Mitchell, Charles Moore, Graeme Morland, Eric and Maureen
Moss, Elizabeth Moule, John Mutlow, James O'Connor, Laurie
Olin, Stefanos Polyzoides, Victor Reigner, John Ruble, Lucinda
Sanders, Leslie Shapiro, Roger Sherwood, Hadley Soutter,
Douglas Suisman and Joshua White.

Frontispiece
Eric Owen Moss: Paramount-Lindblade-Gary Group complex

Chapter opening illustrations
pp17 Frank Lloyd Wright: Ennis House
pp18 Frank Lloyd Wright: Barnsdall (Hollyhock) House,
firescreen detail
pp 54 Pierre Koenig: Case Study House #22
(photograph by Julius Shulman)
pp 55 Richard Neutra: Case Study House #13, plan
pp 72 & 73 Frank Gehry: Schnabel House
pp102 & 103 Morphosis: Crawford Residence
pp152 & 153 Franklin D Israel: Art Pavilion
pp194/5 Los Angeles seen from Griffith Park

Confronting Autopia   Los Angeles requires periodic examination like a patient with high blood pressure. And because of a growing consensus that it represents an urban typology of the future, the frequency of those check-ups seems to be increasing. While these vary in scope and relevance, few if any test the condition of contemporary architecture there in any detail, or the degree of probability with which it may be assumed that it has any connection with the massive changes now affecting the city. There will undoubtedly be an attempt, at some point soon, to use charts and graphs to trace historical and stylistic cross-currents which, however well meaning and skilfully done, will be off the mark. Good diagnosis requires intuition as well as statistics, and architecture in Los Angeles today is about issues as well as influence. Those issues, in this admittedly selective sectional slice through the LA *corpus civicus* at the moment, seem to revolve around the shifting perceptions of the growing multitudes who live there about the character of their city, and the reaction of the established residents among that group (who seem to qualify as such in an amazingly short period of time) about changes that are out of their control. Los Angeles seems doomed to

Santa Monica Place
Santa Monica, 1986
Frank Gehry

Gehry's Santa Monica Place
shopping mall, like his Chiat
Day headquarters in Venice,
demonstrates that the Los
Angeles building as billboard
typology is alive and well.
Two large department stores
anchor opposing corners of
the scheme, while six-storey
parking structures are
positioned to pin down the two
remaining. The mall's name is
spelt out in large white chain
link letters superimposed on
the south parking structure's
blue chain link screen, which
imparts a frank but minimalist
ornament to its roadside
façade.

legitimacy: the mother of 'edge cities' everywhere
is reinventing herself again, and this time she wants
respect.[1] Her past, however, is predictably
embarrassing, and now persists, to haunt her.

As its most visible and pervasive remnant,
freeways arguably remain the most characteristic
and memorable feature of a city now determined to
circumvent them. As historian Paul Zygas has said:
'Despite the clarity of the gridiron and [the]
prominence of the urban set pieces in Los Angeles'
downtown, neither coalesces in our minds as a
memorable Gestalt. By contrast, visitors to Los
Angeles most often remember its freeways, either
with admiration or disgust. And for better or worse,
it is the freeways (rather than individual buildings,
or grand avenues, or public spaces) that remain
ineradicably associated with Los Angeles. Because
the freeways create the total Los Angeles context and
because they condition the perception of Los Angeles'
architecture, eclectic or not, we must give the
freeways their due.'[2]

If the freeways condition the perception and
memory of visitors, they are even more of a
psychological determinant for the people that must use
them during every day they spend in the city. The local
axiom that everywhere you go in Los Angeles takes at
least half an hour by car, should be extended to include
the guarantee that the majority of that time will be
spent on the freeway. Reyner Banham, in his now
canonical *Los Angeles: The Architecture of Four
Ecologies*, defined these 'ecologies' as 'Surfurbia',
'Foothills', 'The Plains of Id' and 'Autopia'. The last of
these he felt to be an unavoidable category in any
description of Los Angeles, because of the 'sheer
vastness of the movement pattern' in the city, and the
predominance of the freeways. As Banham describes
them: 'There seem to be two major reasons for their
dominance in the city image of Los Angeles and both
are aspects of their inescapability; firstly that they are
so vast that you cannot help seeing them, and secondly,
that there appears no alternative means of movement
and you cannot help using them.'[3] There was once a
time, before these gargantuan, contemporary
aqueducts were layered onto the constellation of cities
over which they pass, when people actually depended

Marlboro Man Billboard
A cardboard cowboy in the land of the celluloid hero. The houses in the Hollywood Hills beyond are billboards of another kind, presenting their owners' wealth and taste to the world.

Kentucky Fried Chicken
Western Avenue, 1990
Grinstein & Daniels
In the capital of instant
gratification, fast food outlets
are important enough to be
given special architectural
treatment. The Kentucky Fried
Chicken on Western Avenue,
or KFC, now that no one in
health-conscious LA will use
the word 'fried', is a palace
among drive-throughs, in the
grand tradition of the Donut
Hole, 1968, or the Tail o' the
Pup, 1938. The discernible
shift here, without according
more significance than
necessary to this example of
the genre, is that a client
known for pragmatism has
been willing to move beyond
market tested metaphors into
another realm of design, in the
belief that it would bring in
more business.

upon what are now known as 'surface' streets. These landmarks, permitting a sense of sequential passage through contiguous residential areas, once allowed a unified mental image of an urban texture to be retained, even if that texture was more grainy than most. This sense has now been destroyed by freeways, which only connect with the neighbourhoods below them at major intersections, thus reducing entire communities to a name on an exit sign, and the experience of visual interaction to one of channelled speed, where other cars are the only remaining reference. The disturbing thing is that successive generations have now made freeways the conveyance of choice, and now a majority of time-conscious Angelenos see 'surface' streets as an annoying waste of precious seconds. There are certain times during rush hours, when the freeways are so jammed that the cars, with their colour and model eradicated by the low angle of the sun, seem to blend together into a river of molten metal moving slowly in two directions at once. The popular aversion to 'surface' streets is now so strong, and the dependence on freeways so complete, that even the longest, most frustrating, delay is seen as preferable to the staccato indignity of the traffic lights on Sunset, Melrose or Pico, in spite of the fact that they may actually save time.

The freeway has consequently become the one inescapable social experience that all Angelenos share, with rules and conventions all its own.[4] Indeed, these have become an intricate set of social rituals. The anthropologist Walter Burkert, in his well-researched study *Homo Necans*, has shown how ritual preceded speech as a means of human communication. He argues that such rituals have always been employed as a means of ensuring the psychological resolution of potentially debilitating conflicts, thus benefiting both individuals and the community of which they are a part. Ritual, he argues, is a biological behavioural system that has transcended its original purpose and has resulted in the repetition of a series of interrelated stereotypical actions intended to communicate important information about the original experience. Repetition is a key factor because it ensures that the information is not misunderstood, and that the community or society, though clear understanding,

Hard Rock Café

In Los Angeles, catching the attention of the indifferent or traumatized motorist is paramount. The Hard Rock Café in the Beverly Center projects itself in neon.

Gas Station

Car culture in Los Angeles underscores almost all social activity; the regular stop at the gas station is just one more ritual in the repetitive cycle from surface street to freeway and back again.

will not suffer. When suffering did occur in traditional societies, and the community was threatened as a result, the related ritual would be discarded.[5] In the case of the freeway, the threat has come from LA's astounding population growth, a phenomenon that has also shown a significant impact on every other aspect of the region. There are not only many more cars than there were 30 years ago, in a system that is increasingly unable to handle them, but the cultural mix of drivers on it is now totally different. Imagine rush hour in Mexico City, Seoul, Bangkok, Cairo and Istanbul all happening in the same place, in more powerful cars, and that approximates the condition on the LA freeway today. Each of the multitude of cultures now flooding into the city also brings its own peculiar variations of the driving ritual, with hair-raising results. The highly publicized shootings of the recent past have now escalated to more sophisticated techniques, such as 'car-napping' or 'bump-and-stop', in which thieves preying upon drivers whose normal tendency is to stop to exchange paperwork upon the slightest impact, take valuables at gunpoint instead, and usually include the victim's car as well. Regular impulses, such as concern for others in an accident, are now subverted into self-preservation; and competition rather than mutual co-operation is the rule. The result is that the rituals of the freeway are now separated from their historical, sociological function, as a means of mutual support. Because of the high speeds which are now typical, accidents are rarely minor, with horrific results. Cars flipped upside down, catapulted over barriers, totally flattened, or crushed like an accordion are a daily sight, so that Banham's long-range confidence that 'an accident would never happen' to him, now seems like saying: 'I know that people die of cancer, heart disease and Aids, but because it hasn't happened to anyone I know or to me personally, I'm confident it won't.' Rather than off-ramps being like a front door, and the exit from a freeway resembling 'coming in from outdoors', the sensation is now more like coming off a battlefield, and one of relief.[6]

Contrary to the original purpose of ritual, then, as repetition intended for cultural survival, the LA freeway's lane language and rhythm of indication – as well as the obliviousness to others' pain or distress it engenders – is an isolated affair, pointing to the system's decline. This is not to imply that similar systems elsewhere in the world aren't comparable to the freeways, but mass-transit systems have ensured that these are not as integral to urban consciousness and identity, and haven't conditioned social behaviour to the same extent. As Peter Plagens has said: 'Look around you on the freeway: does that bewildered mother of the drooling infant in the tattered plastic child's seat want to be a rally driver two hours a day? Or the pensioner in the 20-year- old Plymouth? Or the tired shop foreman grinding home after a day near the furnaces? If they had a choice: hell no. But the presiding spirits of Los Angeles ... say you gotta. You gotta until someone comes through the divider and crushes your legs, or until you move to Oregon, or until as seems more likely everyday, you simply cough yourself to death with everybody else."[7]

Because of today's higher speeds, closer tolerances and greater frequency of lane changes, levels of concentration have had to increase, obviating any possibility of freeway architecture, as first proposed by Robert Venturi more than 30 years ago. The few existing examples of this, such as John Aleksich Associates' Arlington office complex, succeed only because they conform to the split-second, freeze-frame limitations that such concentration imposes. Barton Phelps has put forward the idea that a new building type, similar to Venturi's billboard-like Football Hall of Fame, could conceivably undo the damage wrought by freeways layered over 'surface streets', and the disjunction of communities that has been the result. The image presented is of alternating blocks of flats and offices with flat, vertical surfaces, fronting onto the freeway, which could presumably be rented out for advertisements. In reality, such architecture, which is improbable because of the noise and pollution that freeways generate, is only possible on surface streets where lower speeds and stop lights allow time for reading. The building as billboard typology, which has a venerable, 70-year history in Los Angeles, continues to thrive on these streets, and economic prerogatives will ensure that they continue to do so. The Kentucky Fried Chicken outlet on Western

Boulevard, Beverly Hills
The palm-lined antithesis to
the freeway par excellence.

Arlington Avenue Offices
Santa Monica Freeway, 1987
John Aleksich Associates
Stretched out along the crest
of a hill along the Santa
Monica Freeway, near Western
Avenue, this office complex is
one of the best examples of
recent roadside architecture,
because it is carefully
considered, and simply stated,
without inducing sensory
overload. By repressing the
usual commercial urge to build
another amorphous vertical
tower, Aleksich has made a
valuable contribution to the
otherwise relentless concrete
landscape of the freeway,
which may serve as a
prototype for those who
advocate using the land on
both sides of the road to better
advantage.

Avenue, by Grinstein & Daniels Associates, Frank
Gehry's Santa Monica Place and his new Chiat Day
Headquarters in Venice, demonstrate that the
typology is alive and well, and will continue to
thrive in the city as the freeways disintegrate, since
a growing consensus of their obsolescence among
public authorities makes the possibility of any
further improvement unlikely in the future.

As current ambivalence toward the freeway as
a viable typology suggests, Los Angeles elusively
resists categorization, just as stubbornly as it defies
centralization: in spite of an increasing number of
attempts to do both. Yet certain constants emerge
which, when slightly adjusted and fine-tuned to
compensate for the velocity of change that typifies
this city, can begin to establish some boundaries of
a contemporary condition.

The dichotomy between the artificial and the
natural, as one of the most consistent of these,
persists because environmental and geological
extremes are an obvious fact of daily life. As Carey
McWilliams has said: 'The climate of Southern
California is palpable, a commodity that can be
labelled, priced and marketed. It is not something

that you talk about, or guess about. On the contrary,
it is the most consistent, the least paradoxical factor
in the environment. Unlike climates the world over,
it is predictable to the point of monotony. In its air-
conditioned equality, it might be called "artificial".'[8]
Protected by the San Jacinto and San Bernardino
mountains, and the Tehahapi range, joining the
Sierra Nevada and coastal ranges to create a micro-
climate that responds to the evaporative cycles of the
Pacific, this region is the fortunate beneficiary of a
geographical accident. The trade-off for all this
natural bounty, of course, is the San Andreas fault,
and periodic seismic reminders that active, tectonic
plates are in motion. The gradual process of
sublimation that seems to characterize most attitudes
towards the best and worst aspects of the
environment – the persistent sunshine and body heat
temperatures on the one hand, and torrential
rainstorms and devastating earthquakes on the other
– may take place imperceptibly, but it does take
place. Visitors or newcomers, however, who are not
yet infected by this essential *ennui*, are either
overwhelmed by the natural beauty around them, or
slightly debilitated by fear – or both.

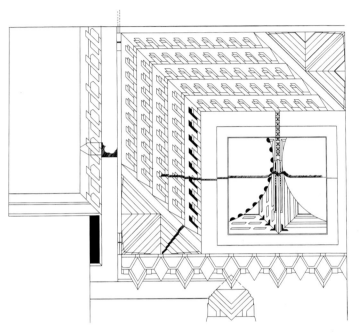

Precedents and Continuities: Putting down Roots

The popular image of Los Angeles is that of a far-flung urban conurbation, with many centres, that have sprung up *de novo* in response to the car culture that generated them, with isolated buildings put up by entrepreneurs seeking to capitalize on proximity to an off-ramp or intersection. While there is some truth in this, a closer study reveals that historical precedents abound, and in a majority of cases the most perceptive, and enduring, architectural statements in the past have been made by those who have come to the city from elsewhere, and have reacted in an instinctive and subjective way to the natural beauty of the region. An identifiable dividing line in debates about contemporary architecture lies in the extent to which such architectural statements are seen as significant in the formation of a new expression appropriate to the region. It is useful, therefore, to begin with a general review of the most significant of these statements.

An attempt to trace historical influence might most profitably start with the Mission Style in California, which began with the real estate boom of the 1880s and was inaugurated by the price war between the Santa Fe and Southern Pacific railroads. As a

reinterpretation of forms used by the Spanish padres who established missions in Southern California, this style was seen as a way to establish historical ties to what was by then seen as a romantic era. The sudden rush of settlers from the east and mid-west, and the just as sudden collapse of the real estate market that followed, generated concern about the image of the region among its 'boosters', and the Mission myth was born. Prior to 1492 it is estimated that there were about 130,000 indigenous Indians in California; when the Franciscans arrived in 1769 there were about 30,000 in Southern California proper.[1] Beginning in San Diego, Missions were established in San Gabriel, San Juan Capistrano, San Buenaventura, San Fernando, San Luis Rey, Los Angeles Conception and Santa Ynez, with the consequence that few Indians escaped the system. By 1910 their numbers had declined to little more than one thousand and, as Carey McWilliams has said: 'So far as the Indian was concerned, contact with the Missions meant death ...

With the best theological intentions in the world, the Franciscan padres eliminated Indians with the effectiveness of Nazi operated concentration camps.'[2] These deaths were due to poor sanitation, caused by the forced removal of entire village populations into Mission compounds, malnutrition, measles and syphilis. Until the 'rancho' period began, and the Missions were finally dissolved in 1848, Indians were virtually slaves to a system that became wealthy on their labour.[3]

The myth upon which the Mission Style was founded – ironically formulated to regenerate a new wave of immigration that was finally to eradicate the last trace of the rancho from this region – was thus of an idyllic, beneficent Utopia, an image which was relentlessly promoted until it became 'California's most conspicuous and influential cultural symbol'.[4] The style was seen as proof of a long and substantial architectural tradition that would rival that of the east coast, and its large expanses of wall and relative lack

Santa Barbara City Hall
As a variant of the Mission Style, Spanish colonial became popular in Los Angeles in the 1920s to the extent that it was adopted as a civic style by Santa Barbara, after an earthquake destroyed the city centre in 1925.

Horatio West Court
Santa Monica, 1919
Irving Gill
Although attracted to the forms of Mission architecture, Irving Gill found them to be too ornate, and determined that they should be abstracted in order to arrive at a more honest style. The Horatio West Court, consisting of a group of four related houses, best exemplifies his highly selective and influential minimalism; the group is made up of flat-roofed units of various heights, with the only hint of the Mission Style being the arched gateways that join them.

of detail made it easily replicable. As David Gebhard has noted, the style was adapted for many building types, prior to the Panama-California Exposition held in San Diego in 1915, which put forward Churrigueresque ornament as a way to relieve its unadorned surfaces.[5] Spanish Colonial, as a variation, also became popular in the 1920s, to the extent that it was adopted as a civic style by Santa Barbara after an earthquake destroyed the centre of the city in 1925. The eclecticism of Santa Barbara's city hall is proof of the inventiveness that was possible in the genre, which continued to prevail until 1930.

Irving Gill, who was born in Syracuse, New York, and had worked with Adler and Sullivan before coming to San Diego in 1893, represents an important transitional figure, having modernized the Mission Style in a way that prophesied the severity of the International Style. His use of concrete over the usual wood frame covered with stucco used in the Mission Style was a significant shift, and as early as 1907, in houses in both San Diego and Los Angeles, he began his clean interpretation of its pueblo forms. His Horatio West Court apartments of 1919, in Santa Monica, which impressed Richard Neutra so much on his arrival in Los Angeles, presage the best of the High Modern that was soon to follow in the region.

As a contemporary of Irving Gill, Julia Morgan had no connection with him other than through her associate Walter Steilberg, who had worked as a draughtsman for Gill prior to coming to Morgan's San Francisco office in 1910. Yet in many ways her work is very similar; it too might be characterized as a more severe version of the Mission Style, at least in the buildings she designed in Los Angeles. Since she has had an important, but largely unrecognized influence on the development of this particular style in the region, equal in many ways to the relationship between the Greene brothers and the generic Craftsman Bungalow, and is now beginning to receive more attention from many local architects, some highlights of her contribution in the region deserve mention. Having received her degree at Berkeley, she was one of the first women to be admitted into the architecture programme there, as well as the Ecole des Beaux-Arts in Paris, which she attended after a brief

Los Angeles Examiner Building
Downtown Los Angeles, 1915
Julia Morgan
The Examiner Building is Julia Morgan's most significant legacy in the city. Built as part of an initial spurt of growth in the downtown area, it occupies a whole block and features a continuous arcade at ground level defined by wide-span arches. The arcades were enclosed as part of alterations made during World War II, but the interior remains intact, its richly patterned tiled floors, exuberant friezes and soaring arched volumes demonstrating the full energy and repertoire of the Spanish Mission Style.

Hearst 'Castle'

San Simeon, 1919-42

Julia Morgan

Morgan's remote palace for William Randolph Hearst at San Simeon, mid-way between Los Angeles and San Francisco, shows her romantic interpretation of the Spanish Mission Style in full sway. The construction of Hearst's 'Castle', as it became known, occupied Morgan for a period of over 20 years, during which time she made more than 500 trips to the site from her office in Oakland, often staying there for days at a time. Its siting is breathtaking: with its axial main building, numerous cottages, pools and terraces, the complex sits on a high mountain crest overlooking the Pacific far below.

period in New York City. During her time in Paris between 1896 and 1902 she also travelled extensively throughout Europe, encouraged by Bernard Maybeck, with whom she corresponded. Her interest in the Arts and Crafts movement, as well as in Tudor, Mediterranean and Bavarian styles began during this period, and was expanded by her passion for books. She returned to Oakland and became registered in 1904, just in time for the San Francisco earthquake of 1906, which provided an opportunity for architects in the city to rebuild it, and brought her many commissions. Her work there demonstrates her mastery of Beaux-Arts Classicism as well as the pervasive influence of the natural environment of her home state, and her attention to the prerequisites of each site.

Morgan's completed buildings run the gamut of types from schools to zoos. All demonstrate a great sensitivity to proportion, scale and materials, carefully related to context, reflecting the influence of the Arts and Crafts movement. The Kappa Alpha Theta sorority house in Berkeley, completed in 1908, is a good example of this connection, having first been covered in redwood shingles, prior to being renovated

in stucco less than 20 years later. The wide projecting eaves and broad vertical masses of the house, which dominates the crest of a hilly ridge, recalls Maybeck, Greene and Greene, and the Prairie School experiments of Frank Lloyd Wright, as a deliberate extension of its surroundings. Morgan's work in Los Angeles, which she produced from her office in Oakland, is limited, but expands on this same theme. The Hollywood Studio Club commissioned by the Los Angeles YWCA is more ornate than previous work, illustrating her response to a different setting and client requirement. The Riverside YWCA of 1929 is also a departure from the relative simplicity of the Theta sorority house, rendered in a Florentine palazzo typology, with a tripartite division into rusticated base, tall unadorned middle and gabled top.

Morgan's residential projects, which are limited to houses for patrons such as William Randolph Hearst and Marion Davies (who commissioned several houses and bungalows) have been compared to those of C.F.A. Voysey in their clarification of vernacular forms and articulation of roof and wall. This clarification has since been widely sublimated, and can be shown to have emerged intact in the work of

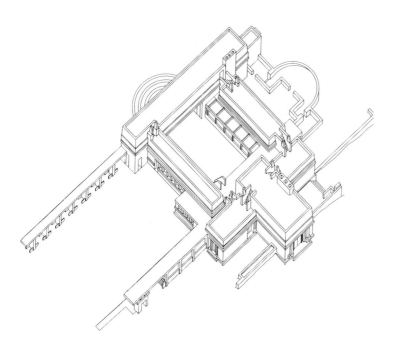

Barnsdall House

North Hollywood, 1921
Frank Lloyd Wright

Of all the residential projects
that Frank Lloyd Wright
completed in Los Angeles
during his brief stay there, the
Barnsdall House is the most
significant in terms of the
position it holds in his career.
As the first house Wright built
in the region upon his arrival
from Chicago, the Barnsdall
(Hollyhock) House provided
him with a means of fresh
creative expression. The idea
for the courtyard came from
Aline Barnsdall, who staunchly
insisted that a Californian
house be equally divided
between interior and exterior
uses, and the roofs of the
residence, as well as the
central atrium, which were
used for entertaining on warm
summer evenings, reflect her
belief.

several of the more historically conscious
practitioners in the city.[6] Although Morgan is
probably best remembered for San Simeon, built
for Randolph Hearst, it is the Los Angeles Examiner
Building of 1915 that for many observers remains
her most significant legacy as part of an initial spurt
of growth in the Downtown area. As described by
biographer Sara Holmes Boutelle: 'The Examiner
Building features wide Mission Style arches, expanses
of white exterior surface, loggias, and skilful
ornamental iron and plaster work. Built on a whole
city block, it enjoys a scale worthy of Morgan's
concept. The arcades were enclosed during World
War II to make them safe during blackouts, but
otherwise the building remains as built. The interior,
with its patterned tiled-floors and ornate friezes, its
great arched spaces with columns and trusses
revealing the structure, flaunts all the romanticism
of the exuberant Spanish-Mission style.'[7] The recent
announcement of plans to demolish the Examiner
Building is a potent reminder of the failure of this
city to recognize and honour the best architecture
of its past.

The plans for San Simeon, begun four years later,
show that romanticism in full sway, carried out in
close collaboration with Hearst himself. The siting
of Hearst's 'Castle', as it has come to be known, with
its axial main building, numerous residential
appendages, pools and terraces, is breathtaking, on its
high mountain crest overlooking the Pacific far below.
The pools, for which Morgan seems to have had a
special flair and which serve as the transitional
knuckles of the plan, are especially well adapted
to the steep contours of the ground, recalling the
flexibility employed in Hadrian's Villa in Rome,
where liquid and solid combine so effectively.

Morgan – along with the other major Bay Area
architects, such as the Greene brothers and Bernard
Maybeck – seems to have possessed an especially
uncanny, almost mystical reverence for nature, which
runs as a continuous thread through each of her
projects as the single constant amidst several stylistic
variations. Morgan's buildings, like those of Irving
Gill, are regional interpretations which frequently
exhibit a pure, modernist, volumetric play beneath

extraneous trim. This tendency is often overlooked by those who remember her for San Simeon alone.

Frank Lloyd Wright, who has had an incalculable influence on certain aspects of Los Angeles architecture today, is prototypical of the overt and enthusiastic reaction to the region's natural beauty that many outsiders have when first arriving there. Between 1917 and 1925 Wright built seven houses in Southern California, and designed at least another 37 projects. His built work begins with the complex for Aline Barnsdall on Olive Hill, which included the Barnsdall (Hollyhock) House, and occupied him between 1917 and 1921, while he was also working in Japan. In addition, Residences A and B, which differed a great deal in style from the Hollyhock House, were also built on the site. Residence A, intended as a guest house, more closely resembles the Hollyhock House, both in its massing and the interplay of the horizontal and vertical planes, but the layering of walls around the exterior gives it a more striated expression. Residence B, also known as Oleanders, was extensively remodelled soon after its completion, and was eventually demolished in 1954, the only one of Wright's houses in California to suffer this fate. In 1921, following the Olive Hill commissions, Wright began work on 'La Miniatura' which was the second home he designed for Mrs George Millard, in Pasadena, and the only one to be realized. The house is generally considered to be one of Wright's most successful attempts in patterned concrete block, with a simple plan that makes extensive use of double-height spaces to offset the small scale, and a purity of massing that integrates it well with its wooded site. The Millard House was followed, in quick succession, by the Samuel and Harriet Freeman, Charles Ennis, and John Storer houses, which were all completed by 1924. Since all three were built simultaneously, in such a short period of time, empirical adjustments to Wright's untested construction system were not possible, with unfortunate results over time. However, the relationship of each of these houses to its specific site, as well as the evident mastery of spatial sequencing, place these among the best examples of Frank Lloyd Wright's work in this regard.

Wright's description, in his autobiography, of his impressions of California on first arriving there is indicative of his instinctive response to the breathtaking contrasts around him. This is particularly evident in his explanation of his design intentions related to the Hollyhock House. Here, he uses elemental analogies to capture universal emotions. His literal and symbolic inclusion of earth, air, fire and water into the Barnsdall hearth, which had previously come to represent domestic security in his Prairie School houses, indicates the extent to which these congruent, natural forces impressed him.

Rather than seeming to slide effortlessly over the earth, as the prairie schooners did on their way through the middle-west, en route to California, Wright's Los Angeles houses achieve the rootedness he himself desired through his use of local stone as an aggregate in the concrete block system he eventually developed, and of native hardwoods for secondary structural members, or trim. Rather than changing material at a subtle and yet unmistakable dividing line between outside and inside, as in his Prairie houses, his use of concrete allowed Wright to do away with the concept of a lining, to evolve a multivalent material that could literally, and symbolically, join nature and shelter together. His joyful discovery of volcanic oya stone – proposed to him by the Japanese craftsmen working on the Imperial Hotel in Tokyo which was being built at the same time as the Barnsdall House, and which could be carved and patterned as easily as soap – may explain the use of similar decorative patterns on concrete blocks in Los Angeles soon afterwards. Wright's contractual obligation to spend a majority of his time on site while the Imperial Hotel was being built only allowed him limited amount of time in Los Angeles during the construction of the Hollyhock House, which caused a great deal of friction with Aline Barnsdall. This friction was the reason behind Rudolph Schindler's having been sent from Wright's Taliesin studio in

Barnsdall House

While Wright's Prairie houses in the middle-west were meant to express the endless horizon, in what was propounded as an indigenous style, their sources were not native to America. In adopting a Mayan profile and ornamental sequences for the Barnsdall House, along with a vernacular, courtyard typology derived from the Mission tradition in California, Wright began to use prototypes more germane to a national past, that would eventually evolve into his 'Usonian' series. The pictogram on the Barnsdall hearth is a coded assemblage of Wright's concept for the Hollyhock House, placed where the four elements of earth, air, fire and water meet.

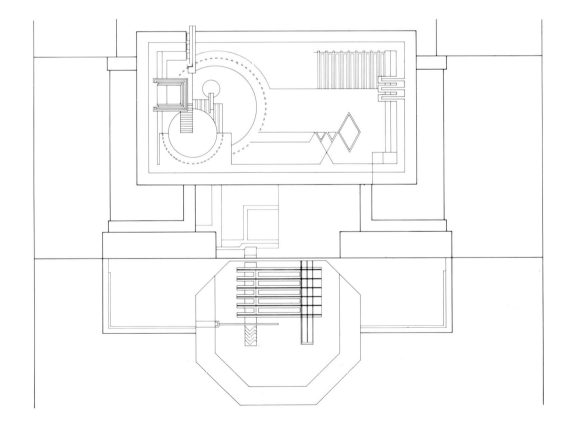

Wisconsin to Olive Hill, since an on-site project manager of such considerable charm was felt, by Wright, to be the only way to assuage the anger of his client and her influential friends.

This eight-year period was the most devastating time of Wright's private life because of the tragic death of Mamah Cheney and her children in the Taliesin fire, his divorce from his first wife, marriage and difficult separation from his second wife, and the death of his mother Anna, as well as that of his mentor, Louis Sullivan, and yet the work accomplished on both sides of the Pacific during this time represents an undeniable turning point in his professional career. Taken together this work contains remarkable innovations and precedents. In his writings about this period, Wright speaks of the Mission Style as an inappropriate expression of Spanish influence, since it had been so diluted by the time it was introduced into Southern California by Junipero Serra. Wright's determination to find a more

native American architectural language, which originally led him to experiment with the Mayan forms of the Barnsdall, Ennis and Storer houses and the North American variants seen in his Lake Tahoe projects, was also the motive behind his development of the textile block system of ornament in a way that would render it truly integral and organic, as well as durable.

Aline Barnsdall's wish to build a small theatrical community, along with a house for herself on Olive Hill, near Sunset Boulevard, was Wright's initial reason for coming to the city, and this commission, which was to have so many implications for other directions that would spring from it, is representative of the direction that his work was to take in the following years in the other projects he was to build in Los Angeles.[8] It is significant in many ways: as proof of his susceptibility to a topography and climate quite different from the central plains, his willingness to search for new and regionally relevant typologies,

Daniel House
Silver Lake, Los Angeles
1939, Gregory Ain

Barnsdall House
The table and chairs in the dining room, and the built-in sofas in the living room, were custom-made for their respective spaces, emphasizing Wright's belief in the necessity of total design. Japanese screens from his own collection of Oriental art graced the living room.

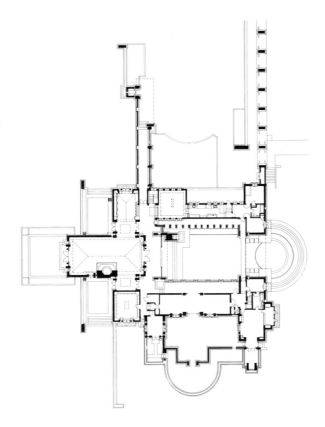

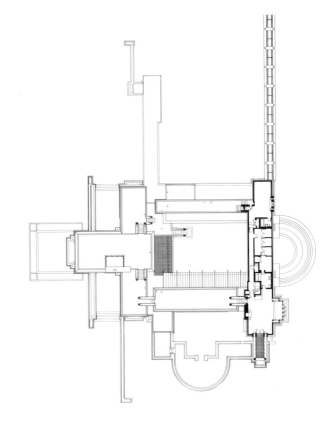

his receptivity to various historical influences and his experimentation with different construction techniques. Whether it was Wright or his client that first conceived the central courtyard of the Hollyhock House is still a point for debate, but even if it was originally Aline Barnsdall's idea, Wright was known never to accept his clients' imperatives unless they coincided with his own. This courtyard, along with extensive terracing intended to capitalize on prime orientation and views, as well as the house's geometric, cardinal relationship with the mountains and the sea, demonstrates the extent of Wright's awareness of an extended natural framework in which the house and its dependencies were placed. The series of 'textile block' houses that followed, in spite of some basic misunderstandings about the bearing capacity of the local soil and the long-term effect of moisture on steel reinforcing bars, is also indicative of a similar kind of understanding of each site, within a wider context.

Wright's accomplishment, during the relatively short time he spent in the region, goes much further than this, however. As Kenneth Frampton has observed: 'It is sobering to have to recognize that Wright's generic house was the last serious effort to evolve and establish a truly civilized typology for American suburban development.'[9] With the exception of the Case Study House programme discussed in the following chapter, the whole progressive undertaking would appear to grind to a halt with Wright's death in 1959.

Wright's death happened to coincide with a series of articles in *House and Home* magazine, which popularized the architect's Usonian notions.[10] The Usonian prototype, which was an analogue for the ideal, American house, was intended to be a democratic answer to popular housing. The textile block houses, which are a permutation of similar attempts to introduce craftsmanship into industrial production taking place elsewhere at this time, also

Freeman House
Hollywood, 1922
Frank Lloyd Wright
Like the Hollyhock House, this house, which was built for Samuel and Harriet Freeman, was conceived as a series of horizontal planes which could be occupied as either interior or exterior spaces, at various times of the day or night. A carefully orchestrated entry sequence beginning with an intentionally long, dark hallway, leads either to the living room, lit by a large, south-facing window that overlooks Hollywood, or to the stair up to the roof, which was intended to function as an outdoor terrace. Downstairs, two small bedrooms open onto another terrace which expands the diminutive scale of the interiors and allowed the Freemans to sleep outside on summer nights.

Millard House
Pasadena, 1921
Frank Lloyd Wright

While similar in appearance to the other textile block houses that followed, the Alice Millard House is significantly different in that Wright used flat metal lath rather than round steel bars between the blocks, and experimented with a cruciform pattern of perforations related to the square planning module used throughout the house. The plans are simple: two rooms on each of two floors, with a stair tower between them, and an outdoor sleeping porch on a third level. The living room is two stories high, with an overhanging balcony, which becomes an extension of the master bedroom.

Storer House
Eagle Rock, 1922
Frank Lloyd Wright
Built in continuation of Wright's
textile block series, the Storer
House uses a smaller module
than that used previously. The
most dominant features of the
house are its stairway, which is
used in conjunction with the
fireplace as a point of
demarcation between the
public and private areas, and
the 20-foot-high windows
which are used to break down
the wall surfaces and diminish
the sense of separation
between interior and exterior.

relied on the Mayan profile – alternately sloping and
flat – used on the Hollyhock House, and an even more
pronounced integration of ornament. Wright saw
Mayan architecture as a truly indigenous, American
style, and a worthy successor to his Prairie School
initiative. While its profile, and its anthropomorphic,
tripartite division, certainly places the Hollyhock
House in this category, later examples in the city show
more direct links to the Mesoamerican tradition,
through their siting and unified treatment of
ornament, thus demonstrating a critical step in
Wright's search for a truly regional architecture.

Wright's Los Angeles houses constitute a
convincing rebuttal of the argument that Bay Area
architects alone really appreciated and responded
to nature. As he later indicated in writing about the
Kaufmann House, Wright actually disliked concrete
because of its inert, inorganic qualities, and yet he felt
the responsibility to develop a prefabrication system
using a readily available, inexpensive material. It is
interesting to speculate on the possibility that, once
he had made the mental leap from the use of natural
materials in his Prairie houses, to a more
representational direction on Olive Hill, Wright was

better able to make the decision to use concrete in the
Usonian houses that followed. The jewel-like design
that came after Hollyhock House provides the best
argument for this theory.

The Millard House ('La Miniatura'), in Pasadena,
which was completed shortly after the Hollyhock
House, is often thought to have been built using the
block and reinforcing bar technique, but it in fact uses
flat metal lath between the blocks rather than the steel
bars used from this point on. A cruciform pattern on
the blocks which penetrates all the way through the
wall is also a departure here. As in the Hollyhock
House, budget over-runs caused the client to rely
extensively on outside advice, which came from the
contractor in this instance. But in spite of financial
difficulties, this small tower in the woods remains one
of his most successful attempts to humanize concrete.
As Wright put it: 'We would take that despised outcast
of the building industry...the concrete block...out from
underfoot or from the gutter...find hitherto
unsuspected soul in it...make it live as a thing of
beauty...textured like the trees. Yes the building would
be made of blocks as a kind of tree itself standing at
home among the other trees in its native land.'[11]

Ennis House
Griffith Park, 1923
Frank Lloyd Wright
As his personal favourite
amongst all the houses he built
in Los Angeles, the Ennis
House is unequivocal as a
statement of Wright's wish to
fuse site and building together.
When approached from its
southern, downhill side, it
seems to rise up vertically as
an extension of the cliff below
it, a unity that is enhanced by
the use of local stone as
aggregate for its concrete
blocks. The entrance to the
house is under a bridge that
connects it with service
quarters, creating a screen
between the street and a
central patio overlooking the
city beyond.

The Freeman, Ennis and Storer houses, built in
Hollywood in 1922-24, all use the textile block
system as Wright intended. The Charles Ennis House,
technically in the Los Feliz Hills, is the largest of these
three, and one of the most stable, since it rises up
from a complex system of retaining walls that fuse it
to the rocky hogback ridge on which it sits. The linear
character of the ridge prompted a design that is
principally horizontal, with various functions
separated by level rather than volume. The on-site
requirements of a system intended to reduce costs
through mass-production proved to be
extraordinarily complex, however. As one observer
indicated: 'The construction of the Ennis House
involved the manufacture of over 20 different patterns
and shapes of concrete block. When combined with
the various different orientations each block could
take, there are more than 80 ways blocks are handled
in this house. Furthermore, the sloping walls of the
main pavilions mean that each horizontal course of
interior and exterior blocks is offset from the one
below. The result completely belies Wright's stated
goal for the textile block of a construction system
which would allow a building to be erected by
unskilled labour.'[12] In spite of such incongruities, the
transition from Wright's earlier handcrafted houses in
Oak Park and River Forest to what he believed at last
to be a viable alternative, is palpable here, with
residual elements such as the characteristic stained
glass windows of that earlier period making a final
appearance in this house. His valiant, if abortive and
impetuous attempt finally to marry handicraft and the
machine may be legibly traced in the transitions that
are evident here, and in his other textile block houses.

The Ennis House represents one of Wright's most
successful attempts to relate a building to its setting.
Contemporary photographs, however, make the house
seem less an extension of its hillside site than it was
when first completed. Again this is due to the problem
of moisture penetration, which causes the blocks to
crack under pressure exerted by the rusting steel rods.
A pale waterproofing applied to correct this problem
has changed the building's appearance completely,
since the aggregate used in making the blocks was
taken from the granite rock of the cliff itself.

Gamble House
Pasadena, 1908
Greene and Greene
As the apotheosis of the American Arts and Crafts Movement, the Gamble House in Pasadena, by Charles and Henry Greene, combines the emphasis placed on the importance of handicraft by English idealists such as John Ruskin and William Morris, with the more compromising attitude toward the machine represented by Gustav Stickley. Completed in 1908, the house is certainly the best known project that the Greenes produced, although many other examples of their sensitive aproach to regional materials and traditions still exist in and around Pasadena.

Craftsman Bungalow

The bungalow has become a generic Los Angeles housing type. Early examples followed models promoted throughout the United States by the furniture maker Gustav Stickley and his periodical 'The Craftsman', which from 1901 until 1916 attempted to codify for Americans the aesthetic imperatives of the burgeoning Arts and Crafts movement.

The circulation sequence through the Ennis House, which typically begins in a constricted entry, is perhaps one of the most carefully choreographed and memorable of any ever achieved by Wright in each of the different phases of his career. A 100-foot-long spine, running the length of the cliff, is used as an organizing device, with a living and dining room as well as a kitchen, guest room and bathroom attached to it sequentially. Various ceiling heights are used to modulate these rooms which, except for the private spaces to the west, seem distinct and yet flow together visually to establish a unified impression of grandeur and elegance not found on the other two houses being built at this time. Changes in the materials intended by Wright have greatly diminished the impact of this spatial sequence, but even in its compromized condition, it is effectively conveyed.

The Storer House had originally been intended as a conventional wood-frame structure in a different location, at a much reduced scale. As in the Freeman and Ennis Houses, windows are an important feature here, considered in a predetermined pattern to stitch interior and exterior together, rather than just being inserted randomly, and this fenestration acts as a continual reminder of Wright's awareness of nature.[13] In spite of problems related to the failure of the textile block system, Wright's Los Angeles houses represent a considerable, comprehensive achievement especially in regard to his sensitive reading of the architectural potential of the region's benign climate and topographical contrasts. His work may be seen to have had an undeniable influence on many architects working in the city today.

Wright's later designs for kit-built houses, executed for readers of the *Ladies' Home Journal*, are also echoed in the bungalow, which was once ubiquitous in Los Angeles. After briefly being threatened with extinction in the early 1980s, it has since made a resounding comeback as a housing type that many now see as a solution to cramped apartment buildings. As Mike Davis puts it: 'There is an emerging movement of younger architects who disown these megalomanic pretensions in the hope of re-establishing a dialogue with their much abused *polis*. They share the insight that Los Angeles possesses a rich, if neglected, thesaurus of design solutions to its problems. In particular, they are rediscovering the wonderful qualities of the Californian bungalow – not just as cheap shelter, but as the building block of attractive, variable-density neighbourhoods. Indeed, the bungalow may be Southern California's most underestimated invention. Melding "multicultural" influences as diverse as Japan, Switzerland and Sikkim, the bungalow was the first mass housing form to celebrate the casual outdoor culture of Southern California.'[14]

The origins of the Californian bungalow, which has a considerable following at present, are obscure, with various entrants laying claim to its invention. What is known for certain is that the type is derived from the generic cottage used by the English in India, its name taken from the Bengali word 'bangla', a reference to the district in which it was first employed.[15] Styles varied according to the climate in which the cottages were built, as their popularity spread; a single-storey structure with raised floor, veranda, and thatched hipped roof predominated in areas susceptible to monsoon rains. Historians trace similar nomenclature in a house built much later, in Cape Cod, Massachusetts in 1888, which was only used during the hottest part of the year, but it does not have the same appearance as the Californian variety. An estate in Boston, designed by Julius A. Schweinfurth in 1896, comes closer to this model, combining elements of the Indian cottage and western model.[16]

Charles and Henry Greene are frequently credited with having used the bungalow for the first time in California, in the Bandini House of 1903, but this was in fact based on the Japanese exhibits they had seen in Chicago in 1893 and San Francisco in 1894, and its plan is not consistent with the type. As R.G. Brown has described their contribution: 'There is evidence that others were building bungalows during the formative years of what is now called the Greene and Greene style. The Greene brothers, rather than being the originators of the Californian bungalow style, appear to have been the outstanding representatives of a broad movement whose less talented and imaginative contemporaries created the "neighbourhood bungalow".'[17]

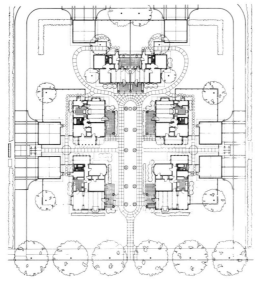

After opening their practice in Pasadena in 1894, Greene and Greene began slowly to evolve a personal style, but only after experimenting with such widely divergent expressions as Colonial, Queen Anne and Mission Revival. Over time, variety began to give way to a tendency toward reduction of surface ornament and a fundamental concern for geometric composition, in an individual rendering of the objectives of the Arts and Crafts movement, modified to respond to the benign climate of their adopted home. Like Wright, the Greenes also sought to marry craftsmanship and the machine, tempering the idealism of English free architecture with the attitude of compromise personified by Gustav Stickley and his belief in mechanized production. While Wright's textile block houses are rhetorical, in so far as they were presented as being mass-produced but were actually constructed from elements made by a laborious process involving a single hand-press, the Greenes present no such paradox, since they managed to achieve an honest synthesis of material, method and craft. The Gamble House, generally considered to be the apotheosis of their work in the Arroyo Seco, is the highest expression of their skill, and is virtually a pavilion from which its inhabitants could enjoy the beauty of their natural surroundings. Wide-beamed, overhanging eaves extend to protect terraces on the north, east and west, which serve as spacious outdoor rooms intended to be used regardless of the time of day, or season.[18] As Edward Bosley has said: 'The Gamble House sits alone in an other-worldly pose, neither a historical quotation, nor seeming entirely new. It represents no social or political ideology, nor a manifesto of design, but gives a glimpse of the pure love of architecture, as felt and expressed by two men who thought less about proclaiming influence on their profession than they cared about celebrating the union of art and craft.'[19]

Attribution aside, the Californian bungalow, in its final configuration, is an indigenous type, unlike others in the state which have been imported from elsewhere. The majority of these were built just prior to World War I, during a period in which pattern books were being circulated and real estate speculation was high. A typical profile includes a

Gamble House

Restrictive covenants enforced by the Westmoreland Improvement Company, even at a time when Pasadena was only a small frontier town surrounded by wide open countryside, limited the siting options available to the architects. And yet, in spite of this, the Greene brothers managed to capitalize on a gentle, north-facing slope, and to make the house appear as if it is inextricably joined to the land. Long low horizontal profiles, also used so effectively by Frank Lloyd Wright in his Prairie houses, help to create this impression, as does the exclusive use of natural materials.

Bungalow Court
Pasadena, 1910

The bungalow court is a common phenomenon in Pasadena. Bungalows are grouped around a central open space, creating a typology which remained a popular form of speculative development until the late 1920s.

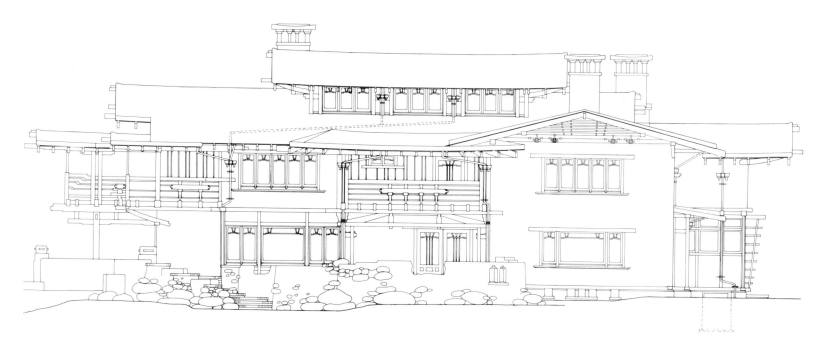

Gamble House

The Greene brothers' Japanese influence is unmistakable in the Gamble House, most obviously in the low overhanging eaves of the gable roof, and in joinery details, where columns, beams and railings meet. Open sleeping porches, extending out from bedrooms at both the north-east and north-west corners, introduce the idea of inside/outside space as integral to a Californian house, an idea later expanded upon by Frank Lloyd Wright and Rudolph Schindler.

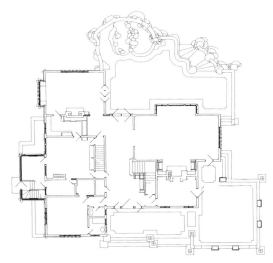

gabled roof with a shallow pitch, with extended rafters, and overhanging eaves projecting over a front porch. Inside, the open living-dining room area usually occupies almost one-half of the floor area, with bedrooms taking up the other half, and a small kitchen near a porch at the rear.[20] Wood is a favourite material, with tar paper or shingles used for the roof.

A variation on the theme is the bungalow court which is now especially ubiquitous in Pasadena, in which a group of bungalows are organized around a central open space. This remained a popular form even after the Spanish Revival style had displaced the 'Craftsman'-inspired bungalow in the mid-1920s, finally having upper floors and open corridors added to transform it into the apartment complexes frequently seen in the area.

In whatever permutation it is found, the bungalow represents a successful attempt to link inside and outside space. In principal, if not material and form, this was also the impetus behind the post-war Case Study House programme initiated by John Entenza, which equally sought to use prefabrication to solve the problem of rapid population growth in Southern California. The work of both Rudolph Schindler and

Richard Neutra, who had what Kenneth Frampton has described as a 'proto-ecological sensibility towards the climate and topography of the region', [21] is especially illustrative of such a link, and is especially rewarding in investigations into it. One remarkable precursor of the Case Study programme, which seems to embody all of the elements later deemed to be essential to a Californian style, is the house that Rudolph Schindler built for himself and his wife on Kings Road between 1921 and 1922. Radical in concept for its time, the Kings Road House was initially intended to be more of a composite than a permanent residence, with none of the accoutrements of a traditional dwelling to tie it to the past. Built soon after Schindler's trip to Yosemite, it incorporated innovative ideas of tableside cooking and common utility – intended to free its inhabitants from a tiresome routine of meal preparation and laundry – and had no compartmentalized rooms in the conventional sense. In a detailed letter to his wife's parents, Schindler outlines his vision for an indoor-outdoor pavilion divided into four main studio spaces for each of its four occupants, which are grouped around two separate, opposite-facing patios intended

Gamble House

Entering the Gamble House from the street is a transcendent experience. Coming in from the glare of the Californian sun, the subdued light and rich colours set this interior apart from its English Arts and Crafts counterparts; its atmosphere welcomes and envelopes the visitor. Sunlight, as it enters this space is filtered and softened by the stained glass panels in the doorway which reinterpret the profile of a native Californian oak to striking effect.

as exterior rooms, rather than having an interior living room in the usual sense. This letter, which is now exhibited in the house itself, is notable for both its conviction and practicality, being concerned in equal measure with both the novel lifestyle that it proposes and the financial feasibility of the entire project. As Schindler says: 'The basic idea was to give each person his own room – instead of the usual distribution – and to do most of the cooking right on the table – making it more a social "campfire" affair, than the disagreeable burden to one member of the family – for special occasions, as well as for all household work which needs expensive equipment ... the "utility room" is provided, containing a complete kitchen and laundry equipment, icebox etc. which shall be used by all inhabitants in common. The utility room therefore, must be in the centre of the structure. The rooms are large studio rooms – with concrete walls on three sides. Those open to the outdoors – a real Californian scheme.'[22]

The Oriental derivations involved, evoked most clearly by the sliding canvas screens and lack of differentiation between inside and outside, are very clear, resulting from Schindler's exposure to the work

of Frank Lloyd Wright both at his studio in Spring Green, Wisconsin, and as his project architect for the Barnsdall House in Los Angeles later on. His awareness of natural surroundings as displayed at Kings Road, together with his innate romanticism, was mostly the result of timing. As Kathryn Smith has so perceptively pointed out, Schindler left Austria just prior to the 1914-18 war and, as a product of *fin-de-siècle* Vienna: 'Schindler took with him elements of the romantic tradition, which for Neutra and his European compatriots were shattered by the violence and poverty of the war and its aftermath. He shared with them the idealism of European Modernism, but while his contemporaries' perception of it was being honed by the horrors of bombed-out buildings and bread lines, his was crystallizing in the sunlit studios of Taliesin and within the steep walls of the Grand Canyon.'[23]

Wright's determination to make the interior courtyard of the Barnsdall House an integral part of all of the interior spaces surrounding it was obviously not lost on Schindler, and this is where the romantic aspect of the Schinkelschule, reflecting the classical connection with nature, is most clear, in opposition

Schindler/Chase House
West Hollywood, 1922
Rudolph Schindler
The house on Kings Road was
designed by Schindler and built
by both him and Clyde Chase
between 1921 and 1922. It
represents an important
historical prototype in Los
Angeles architecture, largely
due to several key principles
that it embodies. As a double
residence, intended for both
the Schindlers and the
Chases, it fully occupies its
100 x 200-foot lot as a series
of partially covered pavilions
directly related to exterior
landscaped spaces, rather
than as a home clearly
delineated by walls, in a more
conventional sense. Through
the use of an ingenious pin-
wheel plan, Schindler was able
to ensure relative privacy for
each family.

Schindler/Chase House

The influence of Frank Lloyd Wright, who employed Rudolph Schindler as a project manager on the Hollyhock House, is obvious here; Aline Barnsdall strongly believed that any true Californian house should be 'as much outside as inside', and Wright was totally sympathetic to such a concept. At Kings Road, Schindler progressively expanded on the idea of the central court used by Wright on Olive Hill, by fragmenting it and integrating individual pieces into the external skin at strategic locations around the perimeter. This penetration is facilitated by the use of sliding, Shoji-like panels, which alternate with concrete lift-slab walls to create a unified language particularly legible in the Case Study House series which followed some 25 years later.

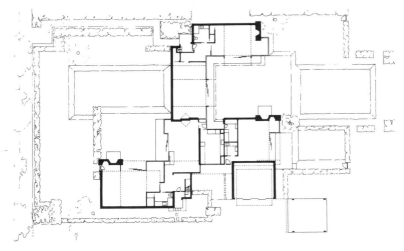

to the distance that Neutra, like Le Corbusier and Mies van der Rohe, placed between their buildings and the landscape. The flipped L-shaped plan used to achieve this integration occurs frequently throughout the surprisingly sizable body of work that Schindler produced in Los Angeles during the 33 years that he practised there, most notably in the El Pueblo Ribera Apartments in La Jolla, which he built with Clyde Chase in 1925. The ingenuity of the Kings Road plan allowed it to adapt well to the changing circumstances of Schindler's life: first as a struggling architect with a young wife and child, sharing the house with the Chases (who occupied the opposite 'L') and then with Richard and Dione Neutra after the Chases' departure in 1924, and finally as the separate quarters of a husband and wife divided by the strain of it all, when a wall built between the two patios permitted joint occupancy with minimal contact.

Aside from the obvious capturing of exterior space that the pin-wheel plan allows, the Kings Road House prefigures the Case Study projects that would follow in its use of industrial materials, modular structure, expressive prefabrication and intentional avoidance of stylistic overtones. It was certainly in Neutra's

Lovell Health House
Griffith Park, 1929
Richard Neutra
As the first steel-framed house realized in the International Style in America, the Lovell House is of unparalleled historical significance. The designation 'Health' House, derives from the fact that Neutra's client, Dr Philip M. Lovell, who wrote a column called 'The Care of the Body' in the Los Angeles Times Sunday Magazine, was determined to be an exemplar of his own regular strictures on fitness, and to build a house that symbolized physical well-being. To this end, he invited his readers to visit him over two consecutive weekends as soon as the house was completed, in December 1929; Neutra himself conducted the tours, which resulted in more than 15,000 people being able to see it personally.

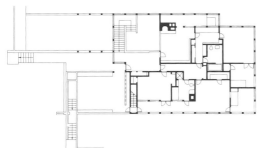

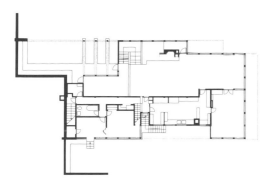

mind as he designed Case Study House #13 in 1946 which, although never completed, shows a specific relationship to the Schindler House, which must have left an indelible impression during Neutra's occupancy there. The lift slab technique used at Kings Road, as well as the narrow module and vertical emphasis of the window mullions, are also recalled in the Eames House which uses a concrete retaining wall tied together by steel reinforcing bars, and a $7\frac{1}{2}$-foot column spacing because of the maximum span of the steel decking used as a roof.

The Kings Road House has today been restored to its former purity, with few omissions to detract from the architect's original intention, allowing a full awareness of the long-term influence that it has had. The dividing wall between each 'L' has now been removed, as has the pink paint that Pauline Schindler used to taunt her ex-husband, goading him into writing long letters of objection to 'Madame' next door. The gardens and hedges, which here are the equivalent of outdoor rooms and walls, have been given equal consideration in the restoration process, in full recognition of the important part that they play in the spatial sequencing involved.

Neutra's residence in the Kings Road House, from 1925 to 1930, corresponds with an important period in this architect's career, filled as it was with new social contacts and the struggle to establish a professional identity in an adopted country. The expansive character of the house lent itself well to entertaining large groups, and during this five-year period it was frequently full of people listening to music and talking about the growing cultural milieu of the city. Schindler's Lovell Beach House at Newport Beach dates from this period, as does Neutra's 'Health House' in Los Angeles for the same client, which was eventually a factor in the rift that developed between the two architects. The difference between these two houses could not more clearly underscore the diametric stance of each designer, and Neutra's distance from the romantic tradition or regional considerations. The former constitutes a directional, portal frame linking building and site, while the latter, for all its highly touted relationship to the environment, is more abstract in its connection to nature. A better example of Neutra's acknowledgement of context might possibly be his Strathmore Apartments of 1933-37, recalling the

Lovell Beach House
Newport Beach, 1923-26
Rudolph Schindler

Lovell Health House
The Lovell Health House occupies a pivotal position in the development of American architecture; for example, the Case Study House programme which followed, after World War II, is inconceivable without the popularization of steel as a residential building material, which Neutra pioneered here. The Lovell Health House thus became the model that Neutra's followers, such as Raphael Soriano, Gregory Ain and Harwell Hamilton Harris, would emulate.

abstracted forms of Irving Gill which Neutra so openly admired, most especially in the Horatio West Court in Santa Monica, of 1919.[24]

With the arguable exception of some of the work of Richard Neutra, then, these architects established an unmistakable legacy of Californian architecture as one with a distinct relationship between interior and exterior space. The Greene brothers, Gill, Morgan, Wright and Schindler were the major protagonists, and if Neutra's Case Study exercises are accepted as a continuation of the Kings Road prototype, he may be included in the category as well. The Case Study initiative expanded on this connection, simply using new materials. The historical legacy of that programme alone – which Reyner Banham has referred to as 'the style that nearly' because it almost succeeded in revolutionizing the housing industry in the USA – is so significant that it requires singular consideration, especially since the problem of housing shortage, which it addressed, has once again surfaced in a city which finds itself in the midst of a population boom. The Case Study series ended in a half-hearted attempt at addressing this issue on a wider scale, and this is where the renewed interest in it has begun.

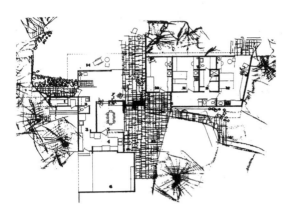

The Case Study House Programme: 'The Style that Nearly' revisited

The evolution of great architecture in Los Angeles beyond the creative legacy provided for the city's elite by Greene and Greene, Gill, Wright, Morgan, Schindler and Neutra, entered a new stage following World War II, when John Entenza sought to restructure its most successful typologies to match upper-middle-class values. This restructuring is significant for us today because it is now being revised as multiple housing for all, as the social agenda of Modernism redux in a city inundated with immigrants from all over the nation and the world. The Case Study House programme, announced in the January 1945 issue of *Arts & Architecture*, addressed a war-weary audience tired of sacrifice, struggle and uncertainty, and quite ready to look optimistically towards a bright new future. As a regional example of the principles of the Modern Movement, it continued to address housing issues through demonstration units of the kind first seen in the 'Ein Dokument Deutscher Kunst' Housing Exhibition in Darmstadt (1901), the Pavillon de l'Esprit Nouveau by Le Corbusier at the Exposition Internationale des Arts Décoratifs in Paris (1925), the extremely influential Weissenhofsiedlung at the Werkbund Exposition in

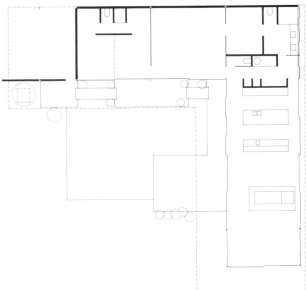

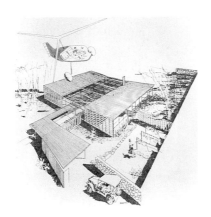

**Greenbelt House: Case
Study House #4**
Project, 1945
Ralph Rapson

Case Study House #22
Hollywood Hills, 1959
Pierre Koenig
In contrast to the delicacy of
Case Study House #21 which
preceded it, the Stahl family
house, which bends around in
an L-shaped plan to occupy
a steep promontory in the
Hollywood Hills, is assertive
and daring. Julius Shulman's
photographs of the house
magically capture the
excitement of the period and
the optimism of the Case
Study programme as a whole.
Seeming to float effortlessly
above the city spread out
below, the house is all roof
and floor, with its glass walls
becoming transparent after
sunset.

Stuttgart (1927), and the exhibition houses produced for the Museum of Modern Art in New York, which became closely identified with the International Style through its exhibition of the same name (1932).

The Case Study House programme had many precedents. What made it most effective, however, was the foresight of publisher John Entenza in using houses that had been designed for actual clients and, in publishing the results, making fantasy believable.[1] Rather than happening *de novo*, the Case Study programme was the logical extension of a continual commitment by Entenza to make the magazine, which he bought in 1938, into an international voice for change, as indicated by the ideological position of its board of directors.[2] As Esther McCoy, who was a member of that group, commented: 'No one single event raised the level of taste in Los Angeles as did the magazine, certainly nothing could have put the city on the international scene as quickly.'[3]

The 36 Case Study projects that were designed and recorded (with a chaotic, non-sequential numbering system reflecting the high excitement and improvisational quality of the programme), fall roughly into two categories: of mixed materials, including wood, prior to 1952, and steel and glass pavilions afterwards. In each case they were intended to be prototypical models of modern architecture for Southern California, sized for middle-class budgets, to replace the labour-intensive houses of pre-war America with an easy-maintenance, carefree vision of the future. Entenza's motives were not entirely altruistic, however. Like his European counterparts, he had total faith in the ability of modern architecture to change popular aesthetics; he had a specific group of architects whose work he wanted to promote, and also he wanted to sell more magazines. And yet he alone managed the difficult task of marshalling all of the necessary resources together to put an idea, then being widely talked about, into action. Reyner Banham relates how Charles and Ray Eames' House #8 came to personify the entire effort for European observers, largely because of the combined impact of both building and furniture, the latter being 'modern' yet far more comfortable than the chairs then being designed by Le Corbusier and others. Beyond

comfort, however, this furniture was impressive because it seemed to embody the pervasive spirit of the time; it was this, rather than its theoretical principles, which made it more comprehensible. Banham uses the word 'confirmation' to sum up the importance to Europeans of the Case Study houses, in that they brought the ethereal and virtually uninhabitable residential visions of Mies van der Rohe down to a more common denominator, while still upholding a fundamental belief in 'clarity, honesty, and unity'.[4]

This comment about the impact of the furniture is interesting because it highlights an important aspect of the programme: its emphasis was on the entire living environment provided by the houses, and not just their envelope. In this brave new modern world to which war veterans would be returning, everything was intended to support a progressive lifestyle and the concept of total design promoted so effectively by Wright and the leaders of the International Style. Other than Richard Neutra, William Wurster, J.R. Davidson, and Eero Saarinen, the majority of the architects chosen by Entenza were little known outside of California at the beginning of the programme. Other, better-known, names were excluded for various reasons, including certain clients' refusal to allow the public visits deemed necessary to get the modern message across. At this remove, however, their collective achievement can be seen as a remarkable act of will, guided by a visionary with exceptionally good timing, and all the more impressive because of its sustained duration.

One of the most famous of the Case Study houses, the Eames House, in fact forms part of a group, or community, of houses built in a flat meadow rimmed with eucalyptus trees at the top of the Palisades, with framed, diagonal views to the Pacific Ocean far below. This group includes the Entenza House and Case Study houses by Rodney Walker and Richard Neutra. The Eames House, completed in 1949, was conceived as a bridge structure of 17 bays of $7\frac{1}{2}$ x 20 feet, connected to a retaining wall stabilizing a steep hill behind it. Of these 17 bays, the house itself uses eight and the open central court four, while a studio takes up the five remaining; the entire composition faces

Case Study House #16

Bel Air, 1953
Craig Ellwood
This house was the first of
three designed for the Case
Study programme by Craig
Ellwood, who came from an
engineering background and
had no formal architectural
training. Ellwood's keenness
to experiment and enthusiasm
for new materials made him
an ideal proponent of the
programme. One of the
smaller Case Study houses
and certainly one of the best
maintained, House #16
is distinguished by walls
fashioned as floating screens,
built as interchangeable panels
set in an exposed steel frame,
whose Japanese influence
is clear.

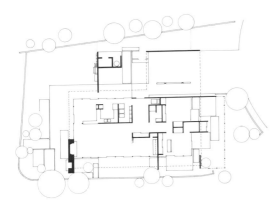

onto the sloping meadow, and looks out through a line of eucalyptus trees which runs in front of all three parts. Last-minute changes were made to maximize the amount of space possible using the steel that had already been ordered, resulting in the openness seen today. As Charles Eames has described it: 'In the structural system that evolved, it was not difficult to house a pleasant space for living and working. The structural approach became an expansive one in that it encouraged the use of space, as such, beyond the optimum requirements of living. However, the actual plan within the system is personal, and whether or not it solves the particular requirements of many families is not important as a Case Study.' Seeing the Case Study lesson to be in the textural aspects of structure rather than inherent in the materials themselves, he continues: 'The texture of the ceiling, the metal joists, the repetition of the standard sash, the change of glazing from transparent to translucent ... all add to the architectural relationship of house to nature.'[5]

Compared with the project's first publication in *Arts & Architecture* magazine in 1945, however, the configuration of the house as built is totally different. Originally its living portion broke away from the hill, on an east-west axis, intended to maximize views towards the ocean and create a natural enclosed compound between the house and the Entenza House next door. The change, from the L-shaped version first published to the west-facing linear bridge attached to the hill that appeared four years later, has been partially attributed, by Edgardo Contini, who helped engineer the first scheme, to its similarity to a Mies van der Rohe house of 1934.[6] The text of its first publication in *Arts & Architecture* stressed the non-typical aspects of the house, and the 'special needs' of the couple that would occupy it, with 'house' meaning 'centre of productive activities' as well as a 'free relation [to] the ground, the trees, the sea – with constant proximity to the whole vast order of nature.'[7]

As finally built, the Eames House uses slim 4-inch steel 'H' columns and 12-inch open-web joists with a corrugated metal roof, covered by insulation board, but the building's true significance lies in the secondary relationship of those materials to space and context. The sense of play with colour, texture,

material and light makes the house seem generous, forming a valuable part of the regional legacy which is still influential today. Here, the strong personalities of Charles and Ray Eames transcend the sense of a rigid system, humanizing it to an extent never seen again in the series. This personal touch extends to the furniture, which Eames designed and had put into production at this time, and to Ray's collections of artefacts, which create tableaux throughout the house.

Following the Eames House, two of the most influential houses of the programme were Case Study Houses #21 and #22 by Pierre Koenig. These fall into what Esther McCoy has identified as a second phase, from 1950 to 1960, when a conscious effort was made to use more steel in the houses, and to make each a prototype. Case Study House #21, which was first published in drawing form in May 1958, was finished later that year, at the same time as the Seagram Building in New York by Mies van der Rohe and Philip Johnson was announced to the press. With characteristic economy of means, Koenig divided living, kitchen and bedroom areas by using an enclosed form that contains two bathrooms and a mechanical room for air-conditioning equipment, making the interior seem much larger than its 1320 square feet. To balance the unrelenting constructional logic of steel (here employed in bays of 10 x 22 feet) Koenig surrounded the house with a reflecting pool, bridged by terraces intended to connect interior and exterior space, and join it to nature. As Esther McCoy has said: 'Koenig handles basic industrial materials with unusual spareness to achieve mobile perspectives. His dispassionate examination of steel is accompanied by an inventiveness of plan and detail, a sensitivity to proportions, and in Case Study House #22 a sensuous feeling for water.'[8] While 'sensuous' may be a bit hopeful, the pools are a novelty in the series in that the water in them is circulated onto the roof for evaporative cooling, and cascades down the sides again through projecting scuppers.

In sharp contrast to the delicate, Oriental, pavilion-like quality of what has come to be called the Laurel Canyon house, Case Study House #22, at 1635 Woods Drive in Los Angeles, completed in 1960, has a more substantial, broad-shouldered feeling to it, due

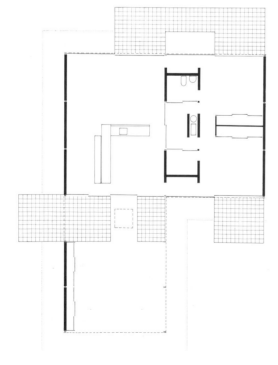

mainly to its reliance on retaining walls stabilizing the edge of the cliff on which it sits, and its wide, overhanging eaves. The owners, the Stahl family, were sensitive to the potential of the site, and realized that a less conventional, open plan would take better advantage of the view. Koenig used 20 foot-wide bays to maximize the amount of glass, providing panoramic vistas of the whole city spread out below. Photographer Julius Shulman, who himself had a house designed by Case Study participant Raphael Soriano in 1950, and had already done much to establish the public view of the programme, photographed the Stahl project in 1960, and in one of those rare instances when that medium manages to distil the essence of a certain time or place, captured not only the physical envelope, but the end of an era as well. As critic Paul Goldberger has described the photograph: 'The house is sleek and white, and its glass walls are cantilevered out over the hills; two elegantly dressed women lounge inside as the lights of the vast sprawl of the Los Angeles basin twinkle below. Modernity and elegance, privacy and openness – things that so rarely went together in the older cities of the east coast – here become one, bound together in a way that epitomized the seductive power of Los Angeles in the first years of its heady postwar growth.'[9] When asked for his view of the Case Study Program, Koenig has said:

The major purpose was to promote Modernism. John Entenza's idea was that people would not really understand modern architecture unless they saw it, and they weren't going to see it unless it was built. The main importance of the programme was that hundreds of thousands of people went through these homes and experienced the principles they incorporated first-hand. There is a broader issue here, too, in the sense that, after World War II, the housing shortage became acute, and many architects realized that it was necessary to design and build in a different way. Prefabrication and mass-production in wood, steel and aluminum, of various components such as doors and windows, increased at this time; with a level of invention not evident today. There was a

heightened interest in determining a process of construction, and yet the process of building houses, en masse, must be economical, by definition. The Case Study House programme only represented a part of what was going on, since hundreds of architects in Southern California and San Francisco were experimenting with similar ideas. John Entenza was astute enough to sense this and do something about it before anyone else did. He promoted this, but didn't start it. His talent was to promulgate ideas that many architects had at that time. My intention was to be a part of a mechanism that could produce billions of homes, like sausages or cars in a factory. In the end the programme failed because it addressed clients and architects, rather than contractors, who do 95% of all housing.[10]

In its exhibition entitled 'Blueprints for Modern Living: History and Legacy of the Case Study Houses', held in Frank Gehry's 'Temporary Contemporary' from October 1989 to February 1990, the Museum of Contemporary Art (MOCA) presented the Los Angeles equivalent of the New York Museum of Modern Art show on modern architecture curated by Philip Johnson and Henry-Russell Hitchcock in 1932, the first recognition of the International Style.[11] The venue in which it was held was an ideal choice for such an ambitious undertaking, envisioned by the curator Elizabeth Smith and installation architects Craig Hodgetts and Ming Fung as a three-dimensional recreation of some of the best models in the programme, both realized and unrealized. In order to engage the audience more directly, the exhibits were produced mostly at full scale, rather than as small-scale one-dimensional images that would inevitably clash with their real, and quite assertive, architectural background. Judging from the reactions of the thousands of people who saw the exhibition, and from the newspaper and international magazine reviews, the exhibition succeeded in its stated aim of providing an objective recapitulation of the successes and failures of the Case Study programme in the light of the new currents of social change now affecting the country.

Case Study House #21
Laurel Canyon, 1958
Pierre Koenig
Case Study House #21 was completed in 1958, near the end of the programme. As John Entenza, the editor of Arts & Architecture magazine, who sponsored the Case Study series, described it, the house is 'a very pristine, clean design. Two details, one north-south, one east-west. One material for the roof, same one for the walls. Minimal house, maximum space.' Surrounded entirely by a shallow water channel, integrally related to an innovative passive environmental cooling system, the delicate structure resembles a Japanese teahouse, and appears even more fragile when compared with the rugged chaparral surrounding it.

House #20
Pacific Palisades, 1948
Richard Neutra

**Entenza House: Case
Study House #9**
Pacific Palisades, 1949
Charles Eames and Eero
Saarinen
The Entenza and Eames
houses were described at the
time of their completion as
'technological twins but
architectural opposites'. Unlike
its structurally expressive
neighbour, the Entenza House
is reticent; a simple 42 x 42-
foot square in plan, its
structural frame and all but one
of its internal steel columns are
concealed behind plaster walls
and a timber-panelled ceiling.
Notable for the flexibility of its
planning and the elegance of
its furnishing, the house is now
threatened with disfiguring
alterations.

The exhibition included walk-in reconstructions of Ralph Rapson's unrealized Greenbelt House, with its potential for finally allowing the modern aesthetic to achieve a physical, rather than simply cerebral, rapprochement with nature, as well as Pierre Koenig's Case Study House #22, and a selection of typical furniture designs to be included in the houses such as Van Keppel's indoor/outdoor lounge chairs, Charles and Ray Eames' moulded plywood furniture and a selection of kitchen appliances. The Eames House itself, probably the most symbolic project in the programme, was also included, cleverly shown as a segment in construction rather than being presented completely; this included a mock-up of its assembly from modular, industrial parts including steel framing, factory sashes, open-web steel joists, plywood and stucco. In addition, the exhibition included a graphic historical time-line of the period, using video-taped interviews with the original architects involved in the Case Study programme, craftsmen associated with it, people who worked with *Arts & Architecture* magazine and the clients who commissioned some of the houses, all presented in a collage format on a curved, corrugated aluminum wall. Twenty-five wooden models of additional selections from the group, built especially for the exhibition, completed the list of displays. Hodgetts and Fung took every opportunity to use the sizable amount of space provided them to good advantage. Capturing the spirit of Rapson's original rendering of the Greenbelt House by packing the garden with 1950s memorabilia, they used a curving aluminum wall as a divider between 'day' and 'night', and placed Koenig's Case Study House #22 at the top of a ramp so as to simulate the view immortalized in the famous Shulman photograph, but had it overlooking TV monitors rather than the twinkling lights of Los Angeles.

What really elevated the show above what might otherwise be considered a trendy nostalgic retake of a period now wistfully believed to be the apogee of American power and prestige, was the concerted effort by the organizers to register the changes in cultural conditions that have occurred since the Case Study programme ended. The exhibition, then, is

significant because it did not merely present the Case Study programme as a historical fact, and its design innovations as inanimate artefacts, but sought to regenerate the ideals it embodied in a widely social context. This was evident in an ambitious invitation given to an international group of architects to create new housing designs for the show. From these, Adèle Naudé Santos, Hodgetts & Fung, and Eric Owen Moss were asked further to refine their schemes, in a competition format, with Adèle Naudé Santos being selected as winner. In collaboration with the Community Development Commission, the Museum also invited Itsuko Hasegawa and Toyo Ito from Tokyo, and Robert Mangurian from Los Angeles, to design prototypical senior citizens' apartments that would be adaptable to mid-rise and high-rise construction.

The exhibition can be seen as a study of a programme which, in Elizabeth Smith's words, was 'a reflection of a certain set of assumptions and developments within culture and society at a pivotal moment in our recent history'.[12] In her introduction to the exhibition catalogue she poses the question of why the original programme did not succeed, and why it failed to attempt to explore multiple housing, as the competition sponsored by the Museum of Contemporary Art chose to do. She also hints at a polemical agenda for the show by saying that, although Modernism has by now been widely slated for failing to meet its self-appointed goals of expressing the technology of the time, 'a belief in the potential of architecture and design to contribute positively to current social needs has resurfaced in contemporary thinking. This belief remains cautious, tempered by the awareness of the complex interdependence of economic, demographic, technological, social and cultural phenomena that shape architecture.'[13] The message of the show, then, is that while Modernism may have failed on several fronts, its social aspirations must be re-evaluated in view of the continuing shortage of affordable housing. It also affirms that the evolution of great architecture in Los Angeles, from houses for the elite by Wright, Neutra, Schindler, Gill, Greene and Greene, and Morgan, through the Case Study houses of

John Entenza for the upper middle class, must now continue on into multiple housing for all.

The three entrants in the competition, who accepted the premise under which it was initially structured with some reservations, show the promise which such a politically correct restriction can provide. By seeking to address those issues now facing architects in the city, MOCA showed the courage of its conviction as well as an admirable willingness to accept criticism of the results. In preparation for the competition the museum convened a panel of experts in January 1987, to advise it on a direction to be taken. As a part of those discussions, it was considered very important to determine why the original Case Study programme, which had originally held out so much promise, had failed so completely. The panel determined that the reasons for that failure seemed to be 'lapses between labour and technology, lack of discourse between architects, builders and labourers'.[14] In addition, they advised the museum

that: 'There is an entire philosophical context of promoting issues of community against isolated units ... changing American life patterns suggest these projects should be multi-family, a community or small neighbourhood that is mixed: singles, single parents, two parents, two parent families, etc.'[15]

This switch of emphasis from the middle-class suburban families who were the clients of John Entenza's architects, to the ethnically mixed low-income groups that now predominate in the city, changed the brief from one of a house, which, as Pierre Koenig has characterized it, could be reproduced like an automobile, to that of an individual apartment that could be multiplied to form a multi-family building. In that switch is described the whole world of encouraging and distressing change that has taken place in Los Angeles during the last two decades. In addition, the experts assembled by MOCA also determined that the competitors should be asked to address 'the isolation, lack of community

Eames House: Case Study House #8
Pacific Palisades, 1949
Charles and Ray Eames
Charles Eames, who along with his wife Ray is best remembered as an industrial designer and film maker, actually produced very few buildings; of these, his own house is undeniably the most influential. Built in conjunction with a house for John Entenza, which is now threatened with massive alteration in the form of an insensitively designed extension, the Eames House was initially intended to be a bridge structure, but the plans were changed after the prefabricated components arrived on site. Rather than placing the building perpendicular to the sloping, northern end of its lot, Eames decided to carve away the earth, and build a retaining wall to which the house is attached.

and excessive cost of accommodation now faced by many Americans, particularity by those demographic groups that the housing industry now serves inadequately'.[16] Faced with this formidable background of requirements, Craig Hodgetts and Ming Fung, who had an insiders' view of the problem because of their involvement in the installation of the accompanying exhibition, chose to divide the programme into eight smaller blocks, in order more easily to adapt to a linear, corner site, bounded by one sharply curving street, at Franklin and La Brea. By doing so they attempted to replicate several communities within a community, complete with interior streets, houses, and 'paseos', arranged in a replicable module seen as a model to be reproduced throughout Los Angeles. This module allowed a variety of permutations and combinations, with the inner street recognized as being an intermediary between the urban reality in the surface streets and the domestic scale directly behind them, an unlikely combination which is unique to Los Angeles. The 'public' face of the complex facing the curved street to the south is open rather than exclusive, or gated, with all pedestrian circulation deliberately guided past a 'community' space so as to encourage resident participation in the supervision of the complex, in much the same way that traditional neighbourhoods in various countries have been designed around a cul-de-sac, to discourage strangers from entering and to allow maximum visibility by all residents. The 'paseos' which lead out from this space give access to each of the central courtyards around which the modules are grouped, providing a second range of open space. The materials used also reflect the change in attitude taken by the competitors, and in this instance stucco-treated plywood and aluminum siding were chosen for their low cost.

In the competition scheme by Eric Owen Moss, who along with Thom Mayne is one of the superstars of the contemporary Los Angeles scene, and has had an enormous influence upon young architects and students both nationally and internationally because of his innovative approach to theory as it relates to the geometrical generation of form, a characteristically novel approach is evident. The Moss scheme took a

Eames House: Case Study House #8

The Eames House's siting creates a protected glade between it and the Entenza House to the south, and allows it to benefit from magnificent ocean views seen from behind its protective screen of eucalyptus trees. The Eames' touches, evident within a rigorous structural system, extend down to the smallest detail, including panels painted in primary colours inserted into the frame, highly personalized furniture, which seems a perfect component of the house, and collections of toys and artefacts from all over the world. The Eames House is arguably the most memorable of the entire Case Study series, since it represents the clearest popular expression of the modern house idea.

somewhat similar position to that of Hodgetts and Fung in regard to an open 'front', strategically positioned at the fulcrum of the curve, to be used as a common, open space, and groupings around smaller central courtyards, but the effect here is more monolithic, as if the intention were to create a single building out of the programmatic requirement of multiple housing. This singularity, however, is decreased by erosions of the solid surface facing toward the south, creating an intentionally ambivalent image intended to allow the complex to relate more easily to its neighbours. The roof forms on various segments are also chosen with this kind of compatibility in mind. Bleachers are incorporated into the smaller courtyards as a metaphorical and functional device for encouraging participation, which has presented great difficulties for architects elsewhere in LA. Rather than specific typologies to be replicated, Moss presents general attitudes toward design, of approachability rather than exclusivity and eclecticism rather than formality. Materials are wood, pressed wooden pulp board, reinforced concrete and drywall, again selected for reasons of durability and frugality.

The scheme by Adèle Naudé Santos, which was selected as competition winner, emphasizes clusters of units, presented as an alternative to what she has termed the 'dingbat' apartment: three floors of wood construction with long, artificially lit corridors, over a dangerous, subterranean parking structure. Instead, Santos breaks down indoor circulation into short, manageable and pleasant stretches, and has tried to approximate the scale of a small town in the way the

components relate to one another. Rather than one 'community' and several other secondary open spaces, covered porches are used to encourage interaction on a more personal level. Like Hodgetts and Fung, Santos uses an easily reproducible module that allows for a number of groupings, but unlike them she sees the modules as autonomous. As she has said: 'Our prototype is the collective environment that supports the residential life of a group of families – an extended family sharing outdoor "rooms" and common facilities.'[17] Reliance on mutual support and sharing, within individual units, marks this complex as a compromise solution, between the continuity of the single object syndrome represented by the Moss scheme, for all its erosions, and the systematic logic of Hodgetts and Fung. It satisfies the architectural urge for individual expression within a clear verbal device of 'sharing', and judging by the positive response that the project received, has also satisfied the dilemma that housing now poses.

The legacy of the Case Study House programme is considerable, and still vital, as the frequency of references to it by people at all levels of interest in architecture continues to indicate. Rather than trying to force the bold initiative that it represented into a preconceived direction, however, it may be that the technological emphasis which was its ultimate failing, as well as its emphasis on utilizing new materials which was its primary insight, might be the place to begin again. It may still be possible to turn 'the style that nearly' into a viable alternative to what is undoubtedly a primitive and wasteful system of wood-stud and wire-nail custom construction

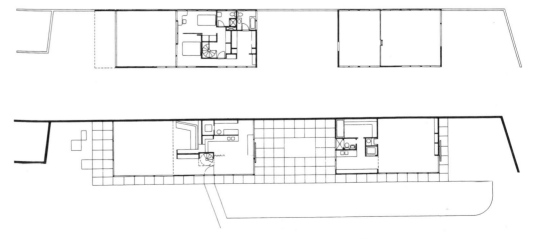

Multiple-Family Housing
Blueprints for Modern Living
Project, 1989
Adèle Naudé Santos

**Blueprints for Modern
Living**
Exhibition at the Museum
of Contemporary Art, Los
Angeles, 1989-90
Hodgetts & Fung
As the first major retrospective
of the Case Study House
programme, this exhibition
represents a reawakening of
interest in the period. The
installation transcended mere
nostalgia for two of America's
most prosperous and confident
decades. By presenting the
entirety of the industrial design
effort behind the architecture,
as well as the history of the 36
built and unbuilt prototypes,
Hodgetts and Fung were able
to convey the real significance
of an initiative that sought to
convert wartime technologies
into a new attitude towards
house construction.

perpetuated by powerful interests. Continuing research and application, as an alternative to the subliminal social commentary hidden beneath an avant-garde architectural statement, could serve this legacy best, rather than patronizing competitions that make broad assumptions about social changes without extensive research. While such shifts have undoubtedly occurred, the final selection made by MOCA – which continues to eulogize the semi-detached suburban house, albeit with a much smaller front yard and crowded covered porch – shows a distinct lack of conviction in the basic tenets of the programme itself. This underscores the confusion that continues to flourish in this arena, and if all architects really do want to be 'housers', as Denise Scott Brown has suggested, it would appear that the ground rules in Los Angeles have yet to be established, in spite of several bold and expensive attempts to do so.

The Case Study programme did not revolutionize the building industry as Entenza had hoped, but the wide media coverage given to it, as well as public exposure through visits, did influence popular taste, easing acceptance of Modernism. Builders, too, were influenced by these ideas, and open plans, relating equally to interior and exterior spaces, as well as extensive use of plywood, glass and prefabricated kitchen cabinets, became the symbol of a casual Californian lifestyle. The transfer from wood to steel in the early 1950s effectively short-circuited the 'Craftsman' tradition of the Bay Area, carried through by Greene and Greene into the bungalow which thrived in Los Angeles prior to World War I, making metal an equally acceptable part of a regional tradition. It would be too easy to dismiss lightly the Case Study programme as a good idea that managed to capture the buoyant optimism of the time, but which ultimately failed because industry remained unconvinced that the systems used could be economically mass-produced. Because its legacy is far too obvious, resistance to change and cheaper alternatives also played a part in the failure of the Case Study programme to induce reform. What can be seen now, however, is that the interest in industrial materials and high technology begun there has gone on to generate an entirely new language.

As this selective retrospective has shown, it is a mistake to consider contemporary architecture in Los Angeles out of a historical context, and there is

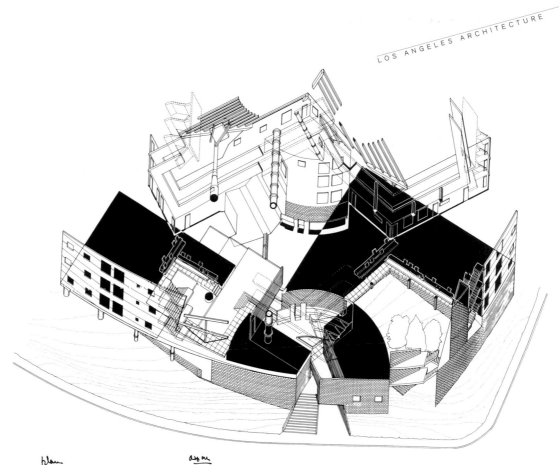

Multiple-Family Housing
Blueprints for Modern Living
Project, 1989
Eric Owen Moss

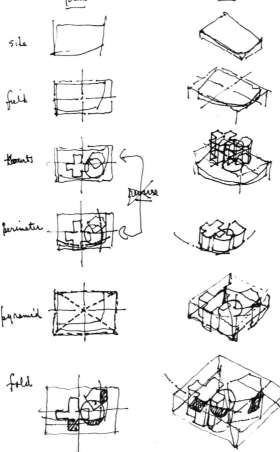

a surprisingly extensive body of work to look to for background. Free spirits, for many different reasons, came here in the past to find a place where they could make a fresh start, or in search of freedom of expression, only to be affected by the overpowering physical beauty around them, which they responded to in remarkably similar ways, that transcended style and more frequently related to regional precedents. While John Entenza's proselytizing fervour prompted the exclusion of historical reference, in true modernist fashion, the need to retain a link to nature remained strong as the basis of a desire to produce a prototype for an American home that would typify the new desire for casualness, openness and easy maintenance that was so important to families immediately after World War II. Just as the Hollyhock and Kings Road houses found fresh adherents among the Case Study architects, who tried to reduce as far as possible the division between internal and external space, to make house and nature one, the architects that follow, to a great extent – in whatever axis they happen to fall – also respond to this tradition, in either a positive or negative way. The possibility of remaining neutral is unlikely.

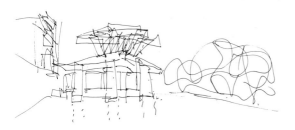

Frank Gehry: Los Angeles and its Discontents

Any discussion of contemporary architecture in Los Angeles must include Frank Gehry, who is the lodestone which others use to navigate whether in a similar, or opposite, direction. At his investiture as the Pritzker Prize winner in 1989, Gehry waxed nostalgic about the past, before his acceptance by the establishment, and in doing so, crystallized several key points about his work that can now help put it in clearer perspective. As he said then: 'It is coincidental but fitting for me to receive the Pritzker Award in Japan. [I was] trained in Southern California in the presence of many works inspired by Japanese architecture, such as those by Greene and Greene, Harwell Hamilton Harris, Gordon Drake, and many others. Some of these were my teachers and they trained us to look at Japanese architecture and understand it. I was seduced by the order of Ryoanji long before the Parthenon, and to this day, I believe these foundations are still central to my work.' Adding to this recognition of Japanese influence, he continued: 'I was trained early in my career by a Viennese master to seek perfection, but in my first projects, I was unable to find the craft or craftsmen, to achieve that perfection. My artist friends, like

Schnabel House
Brentwood, 1989
Frank Gehry
One reading of the atomization
of space in the Schnabel
House has been Gehry's
internalization of the scattered
architectural landscape of Los
Angeles, but a closer analysis
shows that he has intended
this most sophisticated of his
landscape buildings to be a
'metaphor for American
suburbia', which he idealizes
into a small New England
town. Having grown weary of
the uniform cookie-cutter
boxes which have come to
characterize the suburbs of
every American city, Gehry
intended this assemblage to be
an example of the difference
that imagination and skill
can make in the use of
commonplace materials.

Jasper Johns, Bob Rauschenberg, Ed Kienholz and
Claes Oldenburg, were working with very inexpensive
materials – broken wood and paper – and they were
making beauty. These were not superficial details,
they were direct, and raised the question in my mind
about what beauty was. I chose to use the craft
available, and to work with craftsmen and make
a virtue out of their limitations. Painting had an
immediacy which I craved for architecture. I explored
the process of new construction materials to try giving
feeling and spirit to form. In trying to find the essence
of my own expression, I fantasized that I was an artist
standing before a white canvas deciding what the first
move should be. That was a moment of truth.'[1]

This last identification, with his 'artist friends',
may be seen to be consistent with Gehry's ideological
development, which has run parallel to the evolution
of the Los Angeles art establishment since the 1960s.
For many, that evolution began with the landmark
installation of the Marcel Duchamp retrospective in
the Pasadena Art Museum in 1963, by Walter Hopps,
which has been called 'a milestone in twentieth-
century art history'.[2] While this may be a debatable
claim, there is no doubt that this show was the
beginning of an art movement in the city which,
along with Hopps' opening of the Ferus Gallery on
Los Angeles' Cienega Boulevard, helped to encourage
the establishment of a Los Angeles 'school' in this
field. The five years that Hopps spent as director
in Pasadena, prior to his resignation in 1967 and
his move to the Corcoran Gallery on the east coast,
were a time of extraordinary creative activity, and
Gehry was in the midst of it all, listening to, and
absorbing, ideas.

Several experiences during this time had a lasting
influence on Gehry's work, and can provide clues to
his method. A trip to Europe with the artist Edward
Moses, and the overwhelming impression left by the
Acropolis in Athens (which he also referred to at the
Pritzker Prize ceremony), was the beginning of his

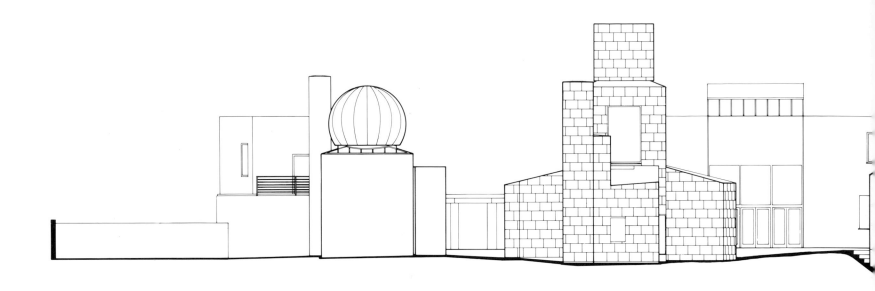

Schnabel House

The village-like arrangement of forms used in this residence, which is located in a quiet, upscale suburban area in Brentwood, was a direct response to a complex client brief, and the architect's wish to create a variety of outdoor spaces that would extend the perception of the size of an elongated lot. This strategy of visual expansion has resulted in different programmatic functions being represented as distinct objects. By varying both shape and surface, these objects have each been given a specific architectural character and are played off against each other.

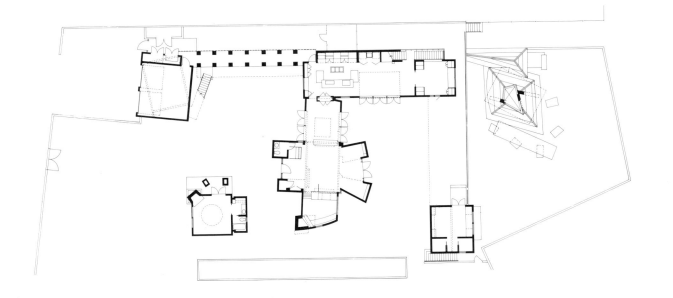

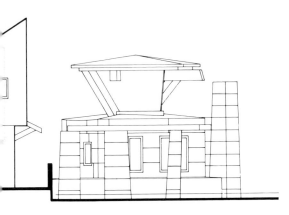

interest in volumetric fragmentation and the architectural village. His commission for the Danzinger Studio in 1964 provided the opportunity to explore Dadaist and Cubist imperatives, and is a Purist construction of the highest order. Much simpler than early Bauhaus experiments with the cube, it is directly connected to Suprematist theory in that it presents to the street a pure, monochromatic composition that is not punctured by a single window. His installation of the Billy Al Bengston exhibition in the Los Angeles County Museum of Art in 1968 is another step in this transition, since it was the first time that Gehry used raw plywood, corrugated metal and exposed wooden joists, pre-dating their more celebrated appearance in his own house in Santa Monica in 1978. The raw vocabulary of the Bengston exhibit was to surface again in even more significant form at the same museum twelve years later, in a presentation of Russian Art entitled 'The Avant-Garde in Russia 1910-30'. Gehry's installation here was particularly responsive to its subject, most especially in his display of the Suprematist works of Malevich, which were based on early photographs of a show called 'The Last Futurist Exhibition 0-10', held in St Petersburg in 1915. His backdrops specifically resemble the rough, abstract stage-sets of Lyubov Popova and Varvara Stepanova, with open joists protruding through the top of flat white panels. In a review of this show that appeared soon after it opened, Peter Schjeldahl attempted to clarify the differences between the movements it presented, and could be talking about Gehry's style as well when he says: 'The variety, complexity and speed of innovation in the Russian avant-garde might seem to defy generalizations, but there are some markedly consistent motifs and tones throughout the canon. What I have called the "alien space" of the movement may be confusing but it does have describable features. This space is diagonal, anti-gravitational and made of light, whether that light is expressed in paint, wood, or steel. From late Cubo-Futurism on, almost everything slants, tilts, cantilevers, thrusts, floats, or launches upward.'[3]

Frank Gehry has been an active participant in scholarly attempts to find the appropriate point of

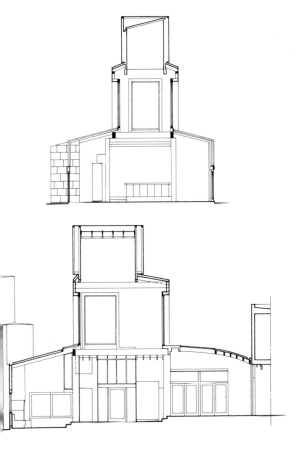

rapprochement between art and architecture, and his unreserved and frequently expressed admiration for artists such as Donald Judd and Robert Irwin continues to provide an important clue to his own self-image. He has often styled himself as an architect whose work has been informed by painting and sculpture, rather than an artist who just happens to build. Gehry has frequently stressed that architects and artists are both concerned with formal qualities and the visual phenomena of the relationships between colour, texture, form, shape and space. He has used his own collaboration with Claes Oldenburg and Coosje van Bruggen as evidence of the discovery of 'common ground', although he is quick to add that it was made only after personal territories were established and priorities were set.

The latest example of such collaboration is his design for the Chiat Day Headquarters in Venice, California, completed in 1989. Located on a long bend on Main Street, the building has been intentionally designed to be roadside architecture, with a one-dimensional, episodic story told along the most visible edge of a six-sided site. Gehry has described his intention here as the need 'to work urbanistically in a community that is practically formless. I wanted it to have differentiation on the street line to break down the scale of the long frontage and to punctuate the entrance with something special.'[4] His choice of an enormous pair of binoculars by Claes Oldenburg and Coosje van Bruggen as that exclamation point reinforces his self-image as an artist-architect. This reputation has been freely acknowledged by Oldenburg who, in discussing their association on Chiat Day, has said of Gehry: 'It was generous of him to give the centre of his façade to a sculpture which is a departure from the usual antagonism between architect and artist.'[5] The beauty of it, for Oldenburg, is that the sculpture is of equal weight with the other parts – which were prosaically named 'boat', 'binoculars', and 'trees' on the working drawings, and are now referred to as such by people using the building – and may superficially be read from left to right, which is the direction most frequently used by cars travelling along Main Street, as a compressed lesson in recent architectural history.

Schnabel House

A cruciform structure, sheathed in lead-coated copper panels, is the focal point of Gehry's compositional grouping, and is located at the fulcrum of the walled, two-level garden. It serves as the entry point to the house, containing the living and dining room, and a library. A three-storey, sky-lit space at its centre accentuates its openness, in contrast to a simple, two-storey stucco volume connected to its northern wall, which contains the private areas of kitchen, family room, and two bedrooms. This appropriately plain building is itself connected (via a copper-clad colonnade) to a garage and the staff living quarters at the front of the site, and (via a partially underground stair) to the master bedroom, which appears to float in the midst of a shallow pool.

Spiller House
Venice, 1980
Frank Gehry
The Spiller House's exterior
walls are sheathed in
unpainted corrugated metal
siding, with raw plywood and
studs used as framing for the
skylight. This gives the
ensemble a rough appearance,
in keeping with the character
of the neighbourhood, making
it one of Gehry's starkest
statements about the use of
cheap construction materials.

In this version, the beloved Corbusian symbol of the
steamship is followed by a superscaled replication of a
commonplace object seen in front of mediocre copies
of the International Style towers in civic plazas all
over the world, and ends with what first appears to be
the deconstructive variant most frequently identified
with Gehry himself.

'Main Street', as it is referred to by Gehry's office,
is an accurate reflection of the rapid evolution and
degradation of the American dream, from the
normalcy and idealism of Sinclair Lewis, through the
commercialism inherent in the Venturi-Scott Brown
dictum that 'Main Street is almost alright', to its final,
artificial canonization in the Anaheim Disneyland,
just a few miles away.[6] As Joel Garreaux has noted in
his discussion of the way that American communities
have changed in his book *Edge City*: 'Disney
produced such resonant dreams that people carry
them around in their heads all over the globe. His
Main Street is a more real crystallization of idealized
community for more people than any nineteenth-
century small American town.'[7]

Gehry's revised version of Main Street recognizes
the drastic changes to the American dream that have
taken place, as well as the dilemma inherent in
working in the rootless context of the parent of all
of the hollow edge cities that Garreaux describes.
Gehry's Main Street is an obvious metaphor for a
historical and physical 'Paradise Lost.' His 'boat'
recalls the Pacific, as well as the elegance of a bygone
era, when Hollywood had style. In the nearly flat
manner of the film sets which still pop up
unexpectedly along the streets of Los Angeles –
converting them into anything from Christmas time
on Park Avenue to a commune on Mars – the 'boat'
appears to be the misplaced scene from a Greta Garbo
movie, needing only moonlight and water to make it
seem real. As a continuation of Gehry's environmental
metaphors, 'trees' recalls the orange groves and the
sequoias once native to this part of California, and the
forests that went up to the sea.

The comparison might even be stretched a bit
further to include an architectural analogy between
the 'binoculars' and the double bell towers flanking
the entrance to the few Spanish mission churches

which still survive in the city, looking particularly
incongruous along Beverly Boulevard. Technically
magnified for contemporary Los Angeles, the mission
gate of Chiat Day now gives pride of place to the car,
with the faithful now relegated to finding their way in
through gaps at the side or along a ramp going down
to the parking level below. The central court is now
the garage roof, with a burl-wood reception desk
adding a surreal note in the half-light of this alien
entry space. So, in spite of Oldenburg's belief that his
'binoculars' have 'equal weight', and play a pivotal
role in the composition, there is something a bit more
subtle going on along Main Street.

When seen from the south, which is when the
tripartite division of the front elevation can be read
to best advantage, the curve of the 'boat' plays a
subservient role, preparing a clear field of vision
towards the two objects next to it, just as does a
similar form in Gehry's Santa Monica Museum. From
this direction, it appears to set up a formal dialectic
between sculpture and architecture, raising interesting
questions about the rapid disappearance of the
dividing line between the two today. In his rendition
of 'trees', which stands out quite clearly as the
terminal part of the composition, Gehry is obviously
caught up in the notion of putting forward his own
entry in this street-side exhibition of sculptural
objects. While it genuflects to its partner and is
similarly divided into base, middle and top, the deep-
red copper cladding used on this office block, which
is reserved for executives at the top of the corporate
ladder, makes it stand out as an object on its own.
This assertiveness is continued in the massive and
angular way that each part is abstracted, with the
profusion of non-structural struts that make up the
'branches' eventually leaving the most indelible visual
impression of all.

The Chiat Day company, which was founded in
Los Angeles in 1968, expanded to offices in New
York in 1980, and finally merged with the Australian
advertising agency Mojo in 1988, looks upon all of
the speculation and attention surrounding its new
headquarters with great satisfaction. This
organization, which deals in images, now has a three-
dimensional logo of its own to identify with and a

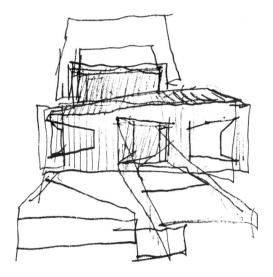

Gehry House
Santa Monica, 1978
Frank Gehry

Few projects have prompted the extremes of popular critical reaction that the Gehry House has. Gehry simply took an existing asbestos-shingled bungalow, in a quiet neighbourhood in Santa Monica, and used it as a testing ground for several ideas he was eager to explore and had hitherto been unable to implement. The result can be seen as an attempt to exhibit the pre-existing bungalow as an object to be carefully regarded, in an artistic sense, in the same way that Duchamp, Schwitters or Rauschenberg used the 'objet trouvé' in their work, and presented it in a manner that forced reconsideration of aesthetic standards and intrinsic cultural value.

Familian House
Project, 1978
Frank Gehry
Designed at the same time as
Gehry's own house, the
Familian residence continues
many of the same themes.
Intended as a commentary on
the process of wooden,
balloon-frame construction,
Gehry expands on the idea of
what he has described as 'the
distortion of the rough wood
tract house technology...into a
tool for sketching with wood...I
was interested in the
unfinished quality you find in
paintings by Jackson Pollock,
for instance, or de Kooning, or
Cezanne.' The extension of
wood studs out onto the site,
as free-form sculpture,
continues this idea, blurring the
lines between architecture and
art in ways which continue to
preoccupy the architect.

pair of binoculars to help visitors find it, all of which translates into a commercial advantage. As with much of the sculpture intended for the public realm today, the real agenda of Oldenburg's 'binoculars' and the 'trees' that answer to them is far removed from the collective enrichment of civic spirit, but has a great deal to do with corporate profit.

In a wider sense, the scenographic, sales-oriented approach that Gehry has taken on Main Street makes it a notable exception to the new direction his work has taken, as well as conflicting with the deconstructivist tendencies ascribed to him. His deliberate decision to collaborate with Oldenburg and van Bruggen here has made this fragmented façade a foregone conclusion, placing Chiat Day in a category defined by Pilar Vilades as a '"Landscape Building" in which various parts, in different materials, are arranged sequentially.'[8] Opportunities to do more monumental architecture have increased in direct proportion to Gehry's international fame, and in the Disney Concert Hall, the American Center in Paris and designs for the Guggenheim Museum in Bilbao there is still collision, but far more unity. While this has partially been the result of functional and acoustic considerations in one specific case, the village landscapes that still surface in residential projects like his iconic Schnabel House are now being consolidated in deference to urban respectability. His buildings now seem to be getting a new suit, of a single cloth, to go to the city.

The Schnabel House, completed in 1989, is Gehry's most convincing residential project to date, the final evolution of several key ideas about fragmentation, inside-outside space, and chaotic order, that he has been working out since his own house in Santa Monica was completed in 1978. Even more important, in relation to a key historical reference that Gehry did not mention at the Pritzker Prize ceremony, is the obvious debt that this house owes to Frank Lloyd Wright. Gehry has made little secret of his admiration for Wright, and as his early Steeves House suggests, that reverence was so strong that at one point he went through a period of open imitation. That influence has now been sublimated into determinations of scale and order, if not detail,

but the relationships between internal and external space remain just as clear. The Schnabel House, for example, may be seen to be a far more subtle homage to the master, with its underlying grid, careful balance between open and closed space, use of clustered pavilions, and specific reference to the grove on Olive Hill, where the Barnsdall House is located. Even if the introductory forest of olive trees seen immediately after entering through the front gate is dismissed as coincidental, the grid, and the open pergolas that result from it, remain to establish the precedent. In this regard, the influence of Wright and his 'breaking the box' is relevant once again, since there are parallels between his Prairie house plans and the way that pieces are connected together in the Schnabel House. These parallels continue in the extension to the outside, which is tied to the house with columns that act like stitches holding the building to the land. The resulting sense of spaciousness required the highest level of skill to satisfy the demands of site and brief.

As cut-rate impressions of historical models, buildings such as the Schnabel House are both representational and non-objective, in direct contradiction to the avant-garde ideal of Apollonian isolation as a posture of self-expression which characterized the Modernist Gestalt. In creating such representative stage-sets, Gehry also implies actors in the best Hollywood tradition, with the architect as the most prominent performer of all. It is no coincidence that Gehry's buildings are a favourite backdrop as movie sets in Los Angeles and, while his paradigm, Frank Lloyd Wright, intentionally sought to create a larger-than-life persona which was so successfully formulated that he was eventually re-cast as Gary Cooper in *The Fountainhead*, Gehry seems to abjure melodramatic theatricality, opting to play the part of architect straight.

Moving beyond Wright, the Schnabel House contains even more basic metaphors. As the most refined of Gehry's 'landscape' complexes, it is a virtual anagram of a New England village, with church, town hall, village green and harbour all taking their rightful place in the architect's idealized mental landscape, presented as his preference to replace the decentralized, anonymous suburb in which it is

Edgemar Development
Venice, 1987
Frank Gehry

Built on the site of an ice cream factory and egg processing plant, the Edgemar complex combines a 10,000-square-foot art museum with a restaurant and retail shops, organized around an open, internal courtyard. As an early example of the Main-Street commercialization of culture, since popularized in the 'City Walk' project at Universal Studios, where UCLA plans to open a storefront branch, Edgemar is a graphic example of Frank Gehry's ability to feel the public pulse, and respond with architecture that manages to be superficial and substantial in equal measure. The central element on the street front is a wall fragment from the former dairy, originally finished in plaster, but now refaced in copper and green glazed tile.

Edgemar Development

Gehry's Edgemar maintains the low-rise, small scale, context of Main Street at this point in what is primarily a commercial zone characterized by small shops and restaurants. The existing streetscale is continued by lining the front of the site with a series of five discrete building elements each with its own sense of identity and placement. Within the site, three towers perform as landmark elements, attracting people into the central courtyard, while their structural lightness and transparency is calculated to interfere as little as possible with the ocean views from the houses on the hillside beyond.

located. Further back on the site, the branches and canopy on the master bedroom 'boat', permanently parked at the harbour's quay, repeat a recurrent dendritic theme to be found at the Edgemar Complex and Chiat Day as well, where fossilized vestiges of earlier, stick architecture recall the forest that once met the sea in California. If trees don't exist, as is frequently the case in Los Angeles, Gehry re-creates them, in abstracted sculptural fantasies. This can now be recognized as thematic in his work.

If Gehry is willing to acknowledge his sources, others are less inclined to do so. In sharp contrast to his homage to the past, 'the kids', as Gehry refers to the generation of architects that have followed him, have been more circumspect about their debt to it; this, however, turns out to be no less direct, in spite of all the verbal subterfuge used to disguise it. In comparison to the Schnabel House, the equally prevalent tartan grid of the Crawford Residence by Morphosis, as well as the emphatic axial orientation of both this and other projects by them such as the Comprehensive Cancer Center, owe just as much to Wright, as several recent geometric studies of the master's work reveal. Seeming like nothing less than a

determined effort to stitch the building to the ground, these spines are one of a series of tactics by Morphosis to claim and hold architectural territory, and when the site is within one of Los Angeles' centres, those tactics escalate to excavation, as a defensive response to superficial surroundings. Instead of the sculpted trees that Gehry has used at Edgemar and Chiat Day, Morphosis use real specimens popping out of a steel container at the Comprehensive Cancer Center, as a symbol of the indomitable will to live or the possibility of normality after chemotherapy, rather than of nature trapped by science; this is part of their on-going dialogue about the appropriate role that technology should play, and a revision of the dichotomy between Schindler and Neutra. With Eric Owen Moss these ties are less immediate, and are now increasingly less apparent as his work becomes more self-referential. Where specific clues, such as Lovell-like portal frames, could be detected earlier on, complex 'emotive' geometries have now taken over, with structural members invented to serve them like new letters in the alphabet of a personal Esperanto. Yet, while this hybrid geometry implies the need for constant change, the emphasis on geometry

Loyola Law School

Los Angeles, 1982-91

Frank Gehry

When Frank Gehry was first commissioned to establish a master plan for the Loyola University Law School, it consisted of one multi-purpose building, and a parking garage. The architect and client decided that the best way to relieve the overcrowded conditions that existed, and expand the campus to serve more than 1000 students in a way that would be appropriate to the educational and budgetary goals expressed, would be through a strategy of phased development. Gehry's first step was to separate the classroom spaces from administration, to allow each to function more freely, and to avoid expensive, long-span construction.

constitutes a search for order, a setting of limits that is as old as architecture itself, placing the work within a chronological continuity of architect as geometrician, a word that may be used to describe both Wright and Gehry. Things change so rapidly in Los Angeles that even its surviving icons, such as Gehry, are now history, and therefore fair game to be quoted. Moss does this in his selection of materials, which are in many instances identical to those used by Gehry. 'The Jeweller of Junk', as Johnson has called Moss,[9] has elevated his palette of constructional detrita to fine art, and much of his design effort is spent on making the commonplace seem uncommon.

On the other hand, architects such as Frank Israel are, like Gehry, far less reticent about recognizing precedents in their work. For Israel, this is related to his belief in the social function that architecture should play. As the most visible example of the proponents of such continuity, Israel brings the argument for a more thorough knowledge of local legacy into high relief, seeing such knowledge as a necessary prerequisite in accurately assessing the hidden agendas of the players involved as the serious game of attempting to establish a dominant architectural language in the city continues.

In the meantime, as the widely acknowledged medium for the psyche of Los Angeles, and sometime muse to successive generations of its architects, Frank Gehry has frequently been categorized as an interpretive formalist, who reinvents his adopted city in each new work. While his subliminal, intuitive and subconscious method initially seems to discourage a deeper reading of intent, several important aspects of its application do emerge as consistent themes. These have, as yet, been overlooked. They go beyond what one observer has described as 'a distillation of the city's own paradoxical variety', involving elemental translations of the critical social, environmental, historical and cultural transformations that are now taking place there.[10]

In addition to his individual renderings of artistic expression, and overt historical references, social commentary has been a consistent factor in Gehry's work and has been amplified by changing conditions. Having begun with the concomitant need to shock

and receive recognition, it must now be measured
against the cyclical eruptions of civil violence that
plague the city, as the primary symptom of a much
deeper disturbance. Unprecedented immigration, and
the social pressures that invariably accompany such
rapid changes in ethnic mix, also suggest that the
ecologies identified by Reyner Banham may now
have to be expanded to a second level of social
consideration in order to arrive at a more accurate
understanding of the city's urban character today. The
discrepancy between the image of Los Angeles as the
model of the American dream, on the on hand, and
the contemporary reality as exposed to the world
once more in the riots of 1992, on the other, will
undoubtedly continue to grow.

This widening rift can be traced in the shift that has
taken place between Gehry's early, iconoclastic work,
such as his own house on 22nd Street in Santa Monica,
finished in 1978, and the political correctness of his
scheme for the Walt Disney Concert Hall, on Bunker
Hill. Partially intended as a personal protest against
the primitive building regulations and construction
techniques that continue to inhibit any real progress
towards standardized, economical housing in the

United States, because of the continuing ability of
powerful industrial lobbies and unions to block
change, the Santa Monica house was at the same time
intended both to ridicule and to elevate the prevailing
builders' vernacular. In addition to being a symbol of
Gehry's acceptance of the limitations of traditional
balloon-frame construction, as well as his frustration
at not being able to implement prefabrication
techniques that would help alleviate the chronic
spectre of ghettos, overcrowding and homelessness in
his native city, Gehry's own house represents his belief
in the expressive potential of the materials he was
forced to use. At the same time it also exhibits several
other layers of meaning relevant to those already
alluded to here. In his *Secret Life of Buildings*, Gavin
Macrae-Gibson has perceptively identified the
environmental analogies that the house embodies,
including the marine imagery of its aqua walls, chain-
link fish tank and rolling lawn, the seismic nature of its
tilted skylight, and its close relationship with the sky.
Macrae-Gibson feels that the marine imagery is
particularly important, since it captures 'that quality
of constant interaction with the sky and of constant
motion so important in detaching the instant of

perception from memory'. He continues: 'Although they are images that concern perception more than memory, they concern only the representation of waves or clouds and not the representation of perception itself.'[11] This preference for perception over memory is important, because it also reveals Gehry's chosen aesthetic inheritance. As Macrae-Gibson explains: 'The concept of geometrical art purely about perception and having no reference to the memory of things perceived is far from new, however, the Suprematism of Kasimir Malevich is its well-spring. If we are to fully comprehend the secret life of Gehry's house, we must examine that profound revision of seeing invented by Malevich around 1913, for it is from Malevich that Gehry's work on the representation of perception can be said ultimately to derive.'[12]

Fredric Jameson has used Macrae-Gibson's insights about the Gehry House in Santa Monica as the springboard for an opposing argument, based on the premise that the work does have a deliberate,

allegorical agenda. In spite of the difficulty of determining whether or not that agenda actually exists, either in this example or anywhere else, Jameson's conclusions in regard to the Gehry House have wider implications for the city itself, both for the immediate and distant future. Jameson respectfully dismisses any Suprematist allegiances in the tumbling cube, translating it instead as a symbol of destabilization; and while he accepts it as an attempt to achieve a state of perpetual shock, he rejects any connections with context. As Jameson says: 'We have refused Macrae-Gibson's account of the symbolic way in which the house anchors itself in its space... Our theoretical refusal was based on the conviction that in a simpler phenomenological or regional sense, place in the United States today no longer exists, or more precisely, it exists at a much feebler level, surcharged by all kinds of other more powerful but also more abstract spaces. By those last I mean not only Los Angeles itself, as some new hyper-urban

City Walk
Project, Universal Studios,
Hollywood, 1993
Jerde Partnership

Chiat Day Headquarters
Venice, 1989
Frank Gehry
Claes Oldenburg's binoculars, in the centre of Chiat Day's main façade, have tended to inhibit commentary on the 'boat' and 'trees' that flank them on the left and right respectively, which have far more substantial connections to the city. With its curved outline, white metallic skin and Corbusian pipe railings, the staff offices have a yacht-like appearance reminiscent of both the glory days of Hollywood and the beach community, with harbours such as Marina del Rey nearby. The dendritic forms of the executive offices, on the other hand, evoke the forests that once stood here, running up to the sea.

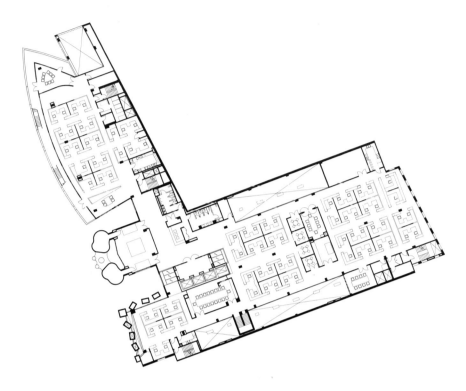

Chiat Day Headquarters

Main Street in Venice is the desanitized version of its namesake at Disneyland, in Anaheim, a few miles away, with both offering a particular commentary on an American institution that has now passed into memory. The idealized version of Main Street, popularized by Sinclair Lewis, as the heart of small towns across the country, has now been swept away by suburbanization and a growing reliance on the automobile, but has been intentionally reinterpreted in these two instances for commercial benefit. Chiat Day picks up the nostalgic theme of a lost idyll, but gives it a particularly localized spin through a selection of metaphors specifically related to Los Angeles.

Camp Good Times
Project, Santa Monica Mountains, 1985
Frank Gehry

Intended for an expansive, wooded site, this camp, which was never realized, was designed for children terminally ill with cancer. Working in concert with artists Claes Oldenburg and Coosje van Bruggen, with whom he also collaborated on the Chiat Day Headquarters, Gehry determined that the melancholy purpose of the project called for up-beat rather than sombre architecture, and proposed an imaginary village of toy-like elements.

configuration, but also the increasingly abstract (and communicational) networks of American reality beyond whose extreme form is the power network of so-called multi-national capitalism itself.'[13] Instead of being contextual, with abstract references to the ocean, mountains and desert nearby, as Macrae-Gibson suggests, the Gehry House in this contradictory reading represents just the opposite, with its tumbling cube intended as a graphic representation of a lack of orientation and its cheap materials an emblem of the economic deterioration increasingly evident in American life today: a symbol of poverty and misery, of people not only out of work but without a place to live, of waste and industrial pollution, squalor, garbage and obsolescent machinery.[14]

In a sense, both interpretations are correct since Gehry, in his own ingenuous description of his intentions in this instance, has mentioned his initial reaction to both physical and social impressions in equal measure.[15] Typically, however, those impressions are carried through intuitively rather than rationally, raising doubts about the validity of any deep reading of the work that goes beyond reflexive

analysis. Gehry has admitted to a desire to 'preserve the iconic quality of the existing house',[16] a gambrel-roofed Bungalow on a quiet neighbourhood street, and to an obsession for having it seem to be 'captured' inside his new shell, so that each part would appear separate, allowing a symbiotic relationship to be set up between them.[17] The exterior shell was pierced and skewed to allow views through at certain points, like framed windows in a Japanese house positioned for maximum effect in looking out at the garden, except in this case the viewer is outside, rather than inside the house. This reversal also provided the architect with a method of commentary on the isolation of his neighbours, who kept shutters and blinds closed, not allowing newcomers to assimilate into the community. This, along with the structural aspects of the house which allude to the unaccountably primitive state of American building technology at the residential scale, make up the 'social' component of the work. But in the aesthetic sense, which Gehry has clearly emphasized as being central to his architectural agenda, the house acts as a metaphor for the middle class with which the architect, in spite of all his fame, still identifies.[18]

Wosk House

Los Angeles, 1984
Frank Gehry

The Wosk House is an anomaly in the Gehry oeuvre in several respects. It is, first of all, one of the few renovation projects that his office has undertaken, and secondly it is more stylistically specific than many other buildings he has produced. Beginning with an existing four-storey speculative apartment block, Gehry left the first three floors virtually intact, using them as a base for a new residence on the fourth. The resulting 'village on the roof' is legible from inside as well as out, with a blue dome above the kitchen and a stepped pyramid over the curved stairway. Uncharacteristically luxurious materials make this a precursor of the more elegant civic structures that Gehry went on to produce.

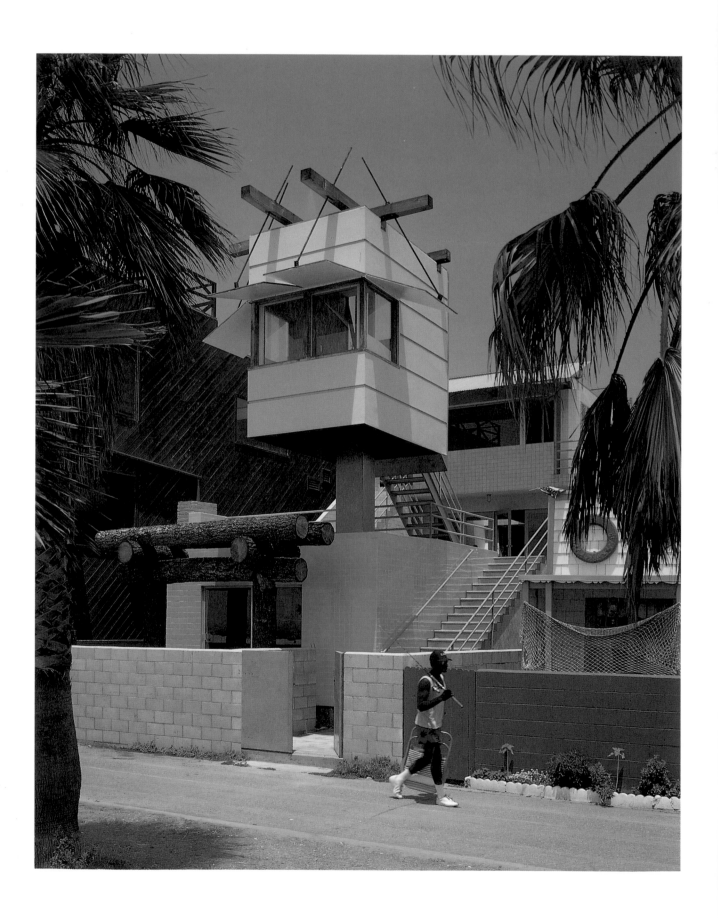

Norton House
Venice, 1984
Frank Gehry

The Norton House appears
at first sight to be a particularly
quirky example of Gehry's
penchant for articulated forms,
divergent, muted colours, and
quasi-literal metaphor. When
seen in the context of Venice's
ocean walkway, however, it
seems almost conventional.
Like the Spiller House nearby,
a relatively modest gesture –
in this instance a studio tower
replicating a life guard station
100 yards away – is used as a
public face to screen the more
private functions of the house
located at the back of the site.
A torii-screen, made of crudely
cut telephone poles, echoes a
culture across the Pacific,
which has consistently
informed Gehry's aesthetic
sensibilities.

To understand the significance of this classification
by Gehry we should look to Clement Greenberg's
classic essay 'Avant-Garde and Kitsch' of 1939.[19] In
it, Greenberg makes the distinction between 'high'
and 'low' culture, describing the avant-garde artist as
one who seeks to protect absolute values, preventing
them from destruction by the masses; kitsch, by
contrast, is by definition non-exclusive, and is
intended for 'unreflective enjoyment'. Greenberg's
evaluation was soon to become a self-fulfilling
prophecy, as art in modernist practice began to be
seen as the last bastion of civilization, a means of
cryogenically preserving its highest values until some
time in the future when they could more safely be
appreciated.

The importance of this point in relation to Gehry's
position, particularly as outlined by Macrae-Gibson,
is not only that it distances him from the modernists
with whom his underlying functionalism would seem
to be most akin, but also that if any parallels are to
be made between his aesthetic and Russian initiatives
following the revolution, they would have to be
with Constructivism rather than Suprematism and
Malevich, since his sensibilities are more in tune with
production for a social purpose than with elitist
isolationism. This ironically places Gehry in
theoretical opposition to artists like Judd and Irwin,
whose work he admires so much. For each of them,
the separation that now exists between art and society
is not cause for alarm, but a necessity, since
epistemological concerns, in their view, must take
precedence over cultural communication. In a
deeper sense, which is more germane to the
significance of his work in relation to Los Angeles
itself, Gehry's architecture can be seen as an
embodiment of the artifice that the city symbolizes,
and of the commercialization of 'schlock', or kitsch,
which drives it.

Few insights about this connection come closer
than those offered by Max Horkheimer and Theodor
Adorno, who wrote about what they called 'the
culture industry' during their Californian exile in
1944, and more particularly about 'the economic
process of selection' which has eventually substituted
appearance for intrinsic meaning as a means of value

judgement. In the final stage of this process, which
now prevails, effect replaces substance, in whole
and in part. The subsequent lack of ideas which such
a mechanism encourages, and perpetuates, creates
a vacuum, in which real life, in the absence of
thoughtful reflection, begins to approximate the
forms of entertainment produced in the city and of
packaging used to imitate it. As a final result, real
experience is measured against the lyrics of a popular
song, a scene in a movie, or an advertisement, and this
actually becomes reality rather than a reflection of it.
The real danger of the freeways, for example, is
trivialized by comparing them to a Disneyland ride;
and the mirror itself becomes a model for further
fiction, since movies themselves are now referred to
as 'rides'. In relating this to the question of style,
Horkheimer and Adorno define artificiality as
something imposed from the outside 'on the
refractory impulses of a form', and there can be no
better description of Gehry's architecture – or of the
work of the 'kids' for that matter – than this.[20] Style,
rather than being an abstraction of life, as it was in
the highest periods of artistic achievement in the past,
becomes a substitute for it. That aspect of a work
of art or architecture which encourages willing
suspension of disbelief constitutes an integral part
of style, and is of necessity devoid of harmony, social
content and particular identity. However, instead of
containing this recognition within it, or achieving
what Horkheimer and Adorno call 'self-negation',
as great art has in the past, much expression today
substitutes imitation for mimesis.[21]

In a masterful refinement of this idea, Jean
Baudrillard has identified the systematic destruction
of reality itself – the inevitable result of this
continuous process of substitution – and its
replacement by what he calls the 'hyperreal'.[22]
Expanding on the idea of copying the copy, he has
identified elements of combination, synthesis, and
total divorce from reality. Within this vacuum, which
he calls 'hyperspace', the imitation implies complete
substitution whereby 'signs' of the real replace the
real itself.[23] The continuity of the past is broken and
the fictive model displaces fact. For a clear example
of such displacement one need look no further than

Gehry's Loyola University Law School, on Olympic Boulevard, which is a stage-set copy of his beloved Parthenon, or his House for a Film Maker, which is a stage set alone.

The implication for architecture in the city in general of this progressive substitution, is that art no longer imitates life, nor life art, but rather art imitates art, as demonstrated for instance by the City Walk project for Universal Studios. Even those considered to be the most accurate and sensitive interpreters of the city are knowing participants in the regeneration of the hyperreal that Baudrillard speaks of. The most significant effect of this turning inward to find the ultimate 'virtual reality' is that the original response to reality, which in Los Angeles is the natural world over which the artificial is layered, has been thwarted and the city's marvellous background has now become invisible.

In relation to Gehry's earlier persona, of iconoclastic rebel and discontent, Victor Burgin has made several allusions to Freud, who has been somewhat superseded by the Lacanian dialectic today but whose observations on social interaction remain valid. As Burgin says: 'One of Freud's books has the title *Civilization and its Discontents*: it contains no utopian prescription for a contented society, its message is that there can be no civilization without discontents. In submitting to the socioeconomic imperative the gratification of the instinctual demands of the individual must be deferred or denied, repressed.' A result of this inevitable process of repression is the formation of the unconscious along with the conscious individual, and consequently, as he says: 'Our self-image, and the images we have of others are always to some degree fictional.'[24]

This relationship between the individual and society has been developed by Lacan as the basis for a theory of psychoanalysis which posits that social values are internalized through each individual's personal development, especially via their appropriation of language, resulting in what he has called 'the dialectic of recognition', being the process by which our self-identity is dependent upon the image that others have of us.[25]

California Aerospace Museum

Exposition Park, 1985
Frank Gehry
Prompted by the prospect of the Summer Olympics, which were to be held in Exposition Park in 1984, the Aerospace Museum was commissioned to serve as an extension of the California Museum of Science and Industry. The concentration of aerospace industries in Southern California was seen as a good reason for locating such a museum in Los Angeles. Its large-scale sculptural forms, as well as the soaring interiors that Gehry has produced, provide a dramatic backdrop for the exhibits, with high seriousness leavened by wit, through a series of colliding volumes that manage to be contextual without seeming to be institutional.

As a means of catharsis which many Angelenos, including Gehry, seem to prefer, psychoanalysis can be seen to serve as a substitute for the social connections of a rural past which many who have migrated to Los Angeles once knew, and is yet another symptom of the insecurity caused by a city that attracts those in transition, as a panacea for rootlessness. While undeniably confining, the legible hierarchy of an established community did provide a greater measure of the Freudian concept of self-identity that Lacan speaks of, and the village-like configurations that have characterized Gehry's designs in the last decade may signify more than a simple, formal preference.

If there is a 'Los Angeles School' of architects and if, as Frank Israel suggests, it is comparable to the 'Philadelphia School' led by Louis Kahn that had its base at the University of Pennsylvania in the 1960s, then Gehry must be its headmaster, and this capacity for self-reference seems to be the only thing that his pupils will admit to sharing with him.[26] Unlike Kahn, Gehry neither inspires nor receives any loyalty from the 'school' he is supposed to lead; indeed his class generally goes to great pains to disassociate itself from him. Neither is he inclined to teach, as Kahn did, perhaps because his visceral, intuitive approach resists pedagogical methodology, or because he has not subjected that approach to the same kind of rigorous, philosophical questioning. As a result, there is no similar body of exegesis available on Gehry's work, which the architect evidently feels should speak for itself since he chooses not to do so, nor are there generations of actual students to carry through his ideas, as there have been in Kahn's case. Consequently, if one would believe the disclaimers of the younger architects in Los Angeles, who resoundingly refute what they categorize as the 'Snow White and the Seven Dwarfs' theory of local architecture, Gehry's role as psyche and muse, if it even existed at all, should be considered very carefully.

**Science Museum
School**
Project, Exposition Park, 1992
Morphosis
Thom Mayne characterizes this project as 'a school in a garden' rather than 'a school in a jungle [the city]'. The new school spans between its famous neighbour, Frank Gehry's Aerospace Museum, and the Corwin D. Denny Air and Space Garden at the corner of Figueroa Street and Exposition Boulevard. It is intended to serve as a gateway into the park and by aligning the classrooms with the rose garden, the hope is that a contemplative atmosphere will result. A stylized 'trellis' extending from the building elevation along this edge reinforces this connection.

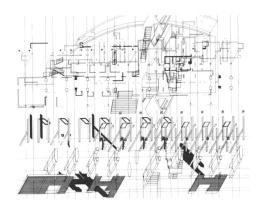

Disregarding Boundaries: The Cult of Individuality

The various overviews of Los Angeles' built environment that periodically appear, typically overlook the possibility that the city's educational institutions may have something to do with the shaping and polarizing of architectural attitudes, or that those attitudes, in turn, may then come to be identified with the institutions. An understanding of the cult of individuality, which is an important factor in deciphering avant-garde directions in the city, can only be grasped by tacitly consenting that pedagogues, such as Louis Kahn, in his many years of teaching at the University of Pennsylvania, for example, do have an enormous influence on their students, affecting the course of architectural history in subtle and complex ways. Kahn, through his love of history, awareness of cultural context, and formal invention, is now widely credited with paving the way for post-modernists, such as Robert Venturi. These shifts in Modern dogma, which are now taken for granted, are particularly visible in Kahn's later work, in projects such as the Luanda Consulate, the Salk Institute and the Bangladesh Assembly Hall. Given the number of stylistic and theoretical directions now open to students, following in his wake, and the fact

Crawford Residence
Montecito, 1990
Morphosis
Beginning with the idea of a
circular wall inscribed on the
two-acre site near the Pacific
in Montecito, California,
Morphosis began to work out a
reversal of traditional domestic
notions of centredness and
protection, using the periphery
of the circle as a place of
enclosure, rather than the
middle. Continuing a
consistent Morphosis theme,
the building relates to notions
of order and time, and the
relationship of each to implied
global co-ordinates, axial
progression perpendicular to
the major view, and the
encompassing idea of the wall
which reflects a concern for
private ownership and territory.

that young people entering schools are generally very
impressionable in any case, the degree of influence of
any dedicated teacher, once a certain direction has
been chosen, is higher than ever.

The Southern California Institute of Architecture,
the University of California in Los Angeles (UCLA),
and the University of Southern California (USC), as
the three leading architectural schools in the city,
offer a wide range of choice in this regard, with
each representing a different, clearly identifiable
philosophical position that can subsequently be traced
throughout the city, in the work of their alumni. The
Southern California Institute of Architecture, or 'Sci-
Arc' as it is most commonly known, has established
the highest profile of all in the media of late, and so
will be examined at some length here.

The connection between academic institutions and
professional architectural offices in an international
context, in terms of a theoretical or stylistic link
between the two at various points in time, would be
a complicated but interesting study, which would be
difficult to structure, but pedagogically useful. In the
opinion of several observers qualified to make the
comparison, Los Angeles is now exemplary as an

instance of an almost direct transfer between the two,
with recognizable territories, and positions, now
established.[1] Of these, Sci-Arc has staked out an
impressive claim, with the majority of its instructors
now active in critical aspects of the architectural scene
in the city. Sci-Arc was founded in 1972 by a group
who were disgruntled with the status quo, and the
words 'innovative', 'leading edge' and 'unique',
frequently used in its catalogues, draw in students
seeking an unconventional direction. Unlike the
Architectural Association in London, which achieved
similar stature under Alvin Boyarsky, however, its
graduates find little need to re-direct or unlearn their
curriculum in order to survive their apprenticeship if
they decide to remain in Los Angeles, since they find
little discrepancy between teaching and practice, if
they are accepted in a like-minded office. As stated by
director Michael Rotondi, former partner with Thom
Mayne in Morphosis and now principal of Rotondi,
the goal of Sci-Arc is 'to produce architects who are
truly artists and thus inherently subversive'. In
Rotondi's view, 'a dedication to redefining the world
as it exists and to resisting the status-quo are the
fundamental responsibilities of the creative person'.[2]

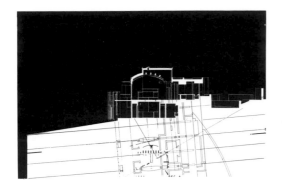

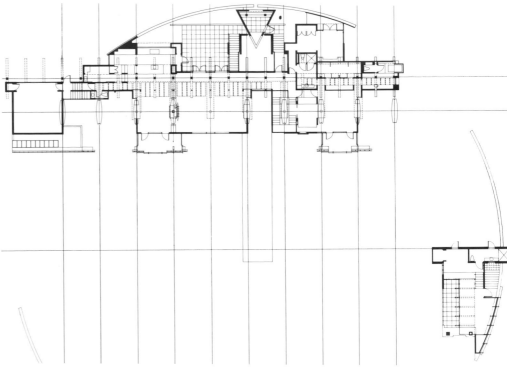

Crawford Residence

The interactive relationship between the building's principal geometries determines the juxtaposition of positive and negative space, creating an implied as well as a visible order within the house. This causes a deliberate tension between elements that are open and closed, present and absent, solid and void. Morphosis' choice of materials – concrete pylons and retaining walls, exposed steel 'T' frames, stucco and redwood for the exterior, and wood, slate and glass block in the interior – reinforce this continual dichotomy.

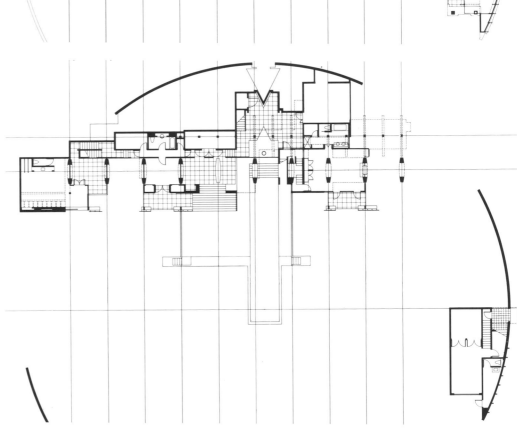

As part of its stated goal of augmenting design tuition with offerings from the humanities, the school makes an attempt to combine fundamentals within a framework for experimentation, with an emphasis on the importance of individuality and the formulation of a singular world view, through the lens of the city, about the current position of the profession. Students frequently refer to a 'process' that they feel takes place here, in the way that the curriculum incrementally leads to a certain stance, raising additional comparisons to other areas of experimentation today. A question that frequently arises in jury discussions with regard to experimentation relates to the fact that unlike other arts, architecture must eventually deal with limits, and construction; theory may contribute to this process, but is ultimately excluded from it, as building returns to the realm of what Kahn called the 'measurable'. Sci-Arc is based upon the premise that experimentation and process are not mutually exclusive, but are as compatible as cause and effect, thesis, hypothesis and synthesis are in scientific method, with the caveat that disorder must now be accounted for and that the concept of linear causality is null and void. The function that theory plays in

experimentation, as it contributes to process, is the issue.[3] The extensive model shop in the new quarters the school now occupies on Beethoven Street, near Santa Monica, is a reminder that craftsmanship and 'the poetics of making' remain an integral part of the process, but student comparisons between this school and the Bauhaus raise doubts about a conscious effort to merge craftsmanship and the machine in this unstructured reincarnation. Because of the way in which the school started, when a high premium, by necessity, had to be put on individual initiative and the resourcefulness of both faculty and students, these qualities are still highly valued, as is the equality of everyone involved in the institution. Such attitudes translate into a highly visible cult of individuality, with a corresponding strand traceable throughout the city, and yet this seems at odds with the post-structuralist alignment of the school. This paradox has been particularly well articulated by Dagmar Richter who teaches there. Rather than seeing architecture as a process, she describes it as 'an initiation of change in a process', denying the possibility of 'timeless' achievement. This conviction stems from her own method of working, in which

models and drawings are used to generate others in
a continuous series of 'translations' by each member
of her studio, each adding a personal interpretation
to them, making single authorship difficult to
determine.[4] The school's success at balancing these
seemingly irreconcilable questions has been evident in
increased enrolments, with new branches now open
outside the United States. Foreign extensions include
Sci-Arc Europe, based in the medieval village of Vico
Marcote in Switzerland, overlooking Lake Lugano,
run from a villa which the school purchased in 1981,
as well as affiliations in Japan, Beijing, Frankfurt,
Turkey and Moscow. These, along with an exchange
programme with the Architectural Association in
London, indicate the international reach that has been
established in a relatively short period of time. The
unasked question that arises in walking through the
smart new Beethoven Street quarters, which are quite
different in character from the school's original
industrial shed home on Berkeley Street, is the same as
the one that comes to mind about the work of Frank
Gehry, who was one of its founding members, but is
not as much of a presence here as he once was. That
question is: will success and recognition spoil Sci-Arc,
which began on a subversive premise? Can 'process'
and 'craftsmanship' and the intuitive approach to
structure which seem to have been integral to the
programme survive the virtual reality of an impressive
new computer room, and can the schism between
theory and form, which seems to be widening, be
resolved? These dichotomies are also those facing one
segment of professional practice, in microcosm:
additional proof that the points of transfer between
school and profession, in Los Angeles, are very direct.

One of the most influential academic role models
in the city today, who has had countless Sci-Arc
students and alumni gain their apprenticeship in his
office, is Thom Mayne, who is now the sole principal
of the architectural practice Morphosis. He was one
of the original faculty members of the school, and
continues to teach there. He has had an undeniable
influence on the direction that Sci-Arc has taken, and
his teaching continues to reinforce his theoretical
stance. Several consistent themes can be traced
through the entire output of Morphosis since 1978,

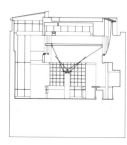

**72 Market Street
Restaurant**
Venice, 1983
Morphosis

Kate Mantilini
Beverly Hills, 1986
Morphosis
As a diner for the 1990s,
Kate Mantilini on Wilshire
Boulevard has the same
rectilinear form, and counter,
tables and booths, as such
venerable establishments have
had in the past, but its 'clock'
indicates the change that has
taken place. In transitory Los
Angeles, regular customers
are a rarity, and the traditional
social focus of the American
diner has been replaced by the
more ephemeral ritual of
seeing and being seen, so that
lineage takes precedence over
substance. The restaurant's
clock is a symbol of the
temporality of the city, and the
shadows on the screen wall
facing the street are an even
more subtle reminder of the
relativity of time inside.

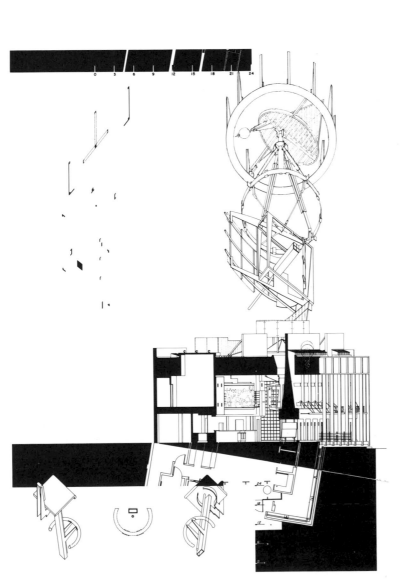

first in collaboration with Michael Rotondi as partner, and then through Mayne alone. One of these is literary allusion, which is ubiquitous at Beethoven Street, and can be traced back to the beginning of the firm's production such as an early project for a restaurant at 72 Market Street in Venice, California, completed in 1983. While ostensibly simple, the Market Street project enshrines layers of complexity expanded in later work, and the Theatre of the Absurd, quoted as its source, has equivalent relevance throughout the remainder of the work that the firm has produced. Structural non sequiturs, such as a central column that holds up nothing but is the armature for everything, begin this line of thought, of a shift from a fixed to a fluid world view in which structure is relieved of the analogous purpose it served in Modernism, and allowed to take on a critical, poetic function. Order remains, and is frequently prevalent, but is intentionally broken to heighten awareness, reinforce symbolism and either encourage or question aspiration. As Martin Esslin has described this particular parallel with the Theatre of the Absurd, it also shows how 'the attitudes and unshakeable basic assumptions of former ages have been swept away, and ... have been tested and found wanting.'[5]

Structure continues to be used by Morphosis as a commentary on the paradox of technology, which today has proven to be something of a mixed blessing, rather than the panacea it was assumed to represent at the beginning of the twentieth century. Morphosis, who use its latest products, focus so intently on details, and have defined structure and its smallest part through such an individualized language, that they obviously do not reject technology. They differ from High-Tech architects, however, in their belief that technology can be used not only to celebrate itself but to symbolize the human condition. The 72 Market Street column, and its heirs in the Kate Mantilini restaurant clock and the tree bursting out of a chemo-quadratic column in the Comprehensive Cancer Center, are *umbilicus mundi,* purposefully intended to root their respective constructs in place and time. While each increases in totemic and mechanical complexity, as intricate machines devised

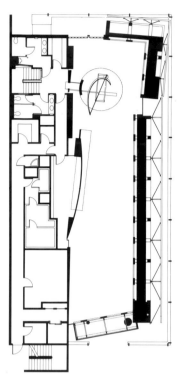

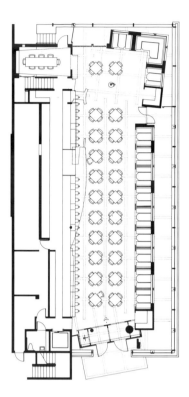

Yuzen Car Museum
Sunset Boulevard
Project, 1992
Morphosis
As a symbolic monument to
the car culture of Los Angeles,
the Yuzen Museum, which is
located on its most sacred
boulevard, not only displays
automobiles, but recalls
parking structures and freeway
off-ramps, in unmistakable,
formal metaphors.

Kate Mantilini
Given the compressed sense
of time in Los Angeles, this
restaurant, which was
completed in 1986, is now
considered to be a historic
landmark. The major reason
for the serendipitous 'fit' is the
exterior columnar grid, which
Morphosis chose to retain from
the existing structure and
which is used to regulate the
new building inside it.

simply for the love of making things (the 'poetics of
making' again), they all have a point to make and a
story to tell, and that story always includes the city
of Los Angeles as the second part of the equation.
Sometimes, where a mechanical sculpture would not
be appropriate or where the scale does not allow an
additional statement, the story is expanded to become
the building itself. In these cases, such as the
Crawford House in Montecito, north of Malibu,
completed in 1990, the axis is invisible but just as
strongly felt, with the house rotating around it like a
chronometer, inscribing the landscape with greater or
lesser purpose at certain points depending upon the
importance of each part. Consequently structure,
which is hierarchical, but fragmented in certain
places, totally takes over this self-imposed mandate,
reading like a stochastic musical score in all
Morphosis drawings.

Thom Mayne is a product of the Ralph Knowles
studio at the University of Southern California, where
a sun machine is a conspicuous part of the
methodology used. Diurnal cycles, shades and
shadows are not only tracked there, but form part
of the architecture itself, with the optimum envelope

being that which not only allows the most sunlight
to penetrate each space at the appropriate time of the
day and year, but also shapes the resulting shadows
in the most pleasing way. Morphosis drawings are
typically tied to the page by structural lines that recall
longitude and latitude, as well as shading patterns
usually descriptive of sunset. Since the Crawford
House was realized, this urge to join building and
landscape together in a more substantial way seems to
have increased, especially in local projects such as the
Performing Arts Pavilion at Arts Park, the Yuzen Car
Museum, the Blades Residence and the Unified School
for Exposition Park, each of which seem to scratch
their way into the ground like a soldier digging a
foxhole under fire.

The wish for unity with surface has always been
implicit in the way that models are made at
Morphosis, with earth and building being rendered in
the same faux-metallic coloured plaster, reminiscent
of the toy-train yards of childhood or the more recent
rage for star-ship miniatures. The model for the 6th
Street Residence, of 1988, is one of the most
memorable. With its custom-made stand, rust-
coloured base and plinth out of which a wooden core,

**Cedars-Sinai
Comprehensive Cancer
Center**
Los Angeles, 1987
Morphosis
An 'intervention' between
three existing buildings forming
part of the Cedars-Sinai
Medical Center, this out-
patient facility combines
diagnosis, treatment and
patient counselling in one
cohesive unit. The new
complex is connected directly
to the existing Medical Center,
and shares many of its
technical facilities, and yet
manages, through consistency
of structure and a uniform
language of materials, to retain
its own autonomy. The most
important aspect of this
design, however, is its physical
and psychological contribution
to its setting and to the
patients that use it. Symbolic
tree sculptures aside, the
entire complex manages to
transform a potentially negative
experience into a positive,
hopeful one.

rendered in similarly-coloured, individually-applied boards seems to emerge like a crystalline eruption, it characteristically goes beyond representation to attempt to achieve the status of sacred object. While also partially buried, because it responds to a pre-existing condition, the 6th Street Residence is additionally intended to fuse with its particular corner in Santa Monica by embodying what the architects describe as 'an imagined prehistory of a place, an archeological past and its subsequent transmission across time. The work aspires to widen one's picture of reality – to evoke disquieting states of mind that prompt one to doubt the impersonal and detached existence of things.'[6] This paradox, between a belief in the absurdity of permanence (especially in a city that has come to stand for ephemerality) and a wish to raise doubts about it, is a critical duality that has been consistently present in the architecture of Morphosis and one which has served to set it apart from others, most notably from that of Frank Gehry,

who holds a mirror up to the shifting face of Los Angeles rather than trying to root it to the ground. Much of this, in Thom Mayne's case, can again be traced back to Ralph Knowles at the University of Southern California, who stresses the importance of the interconnectedness of figure, ground and sky. While Gehry has arguably been more conscious of context lately, as projects following his reconstructed streetscape at the Aerospace Museum in Exposition Park indicate, there is a decided difference in intent. Where Gehry frequently attempts to establish an idealized street or city inside one that is far from ideal in the traditional, monocentric sense, Morphosis builds fortresses which point to the global network now responsible for the present and future shape of the urban fabric.

No better example of this difference exists than the Science Museum School that Morphosis has designed as an addition to Gehry's Aerospace Museum, since, unlike its predecessor, it weaves into terrestrial rather

0°00'   28°31'   60°00'   77°30'

20

10

0

10

20

-24.00

30

6th Street Residence
Project, Santa Monica,1988
Morphosis

**Salick Office Tower /
8201 Beverly Boulevard**
1990-91, Morphosis
This refit of a 1960s
developer's box represents
more of a radical intervention
than is obvious at first sight.
Morphosis identified
fundamental elements which
would not change, and went
about transforming them into
something else: 'We made a
slice at the penthouse which
turned it into the side wall of a
new building, one of two, so
that the original volume
recedes.' The result is two
buildings sitting next to each
other, with the lower portion,
which is the opaque black
glazed building, seen as
conceptually solid, and the
unglazed half, which
incorporates the old
penthouse, as open. Each
become parts of a new,
dialectical form.

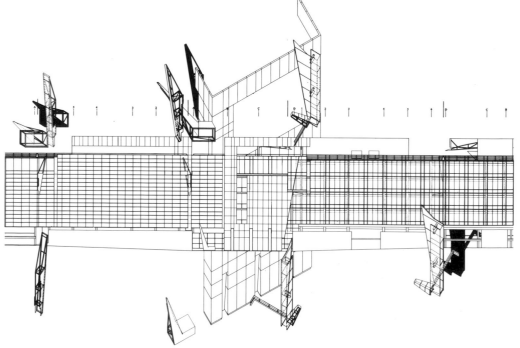

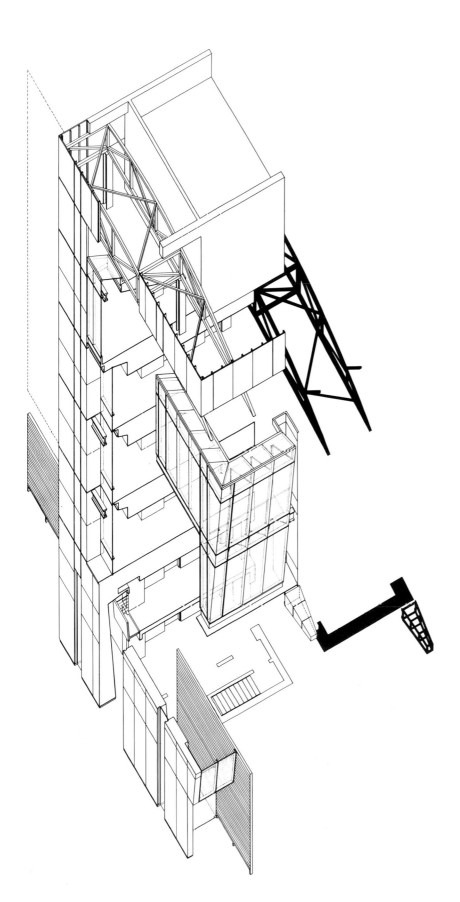

than built co-ordinates. Using the grid of a nearby rose garden as a guide, rather than its illustrious architectural neighbour, the Science School rises vertically from an intricate base carved carefully into the ground, irrespective of the complications this causes for the adjacent museum. This protective stance is partially a result of the fact that Mayne regards Los Angeles with a combination of 'fascination and fear' because, unlike any other city in the world today, it has no ethical or political consensus or majority.[7]

Mayne's own perception of his response to his surroundings bears repeating at length because it has such relevance to the contemporary urban condition, and to the actual mechanisms of assimilation as experienced by a particularly sensitive interpreter. 'One of the issues that effects our work,' Mayne has said, 'has to do with practising in the city and what it represents.' He continues:

At first, the feeling was that the effect was minimal, but as time goes on there is a realization that Los Angeles is a unique place, in some way the prototype of a future metropolis, not existentially, in a positive sense, but in a political-cultural way. This is the only large metropolis in the world that has a minority rather than majority structure, which parallels our search for a paradigm that represents both the larger city and pluralism.

Certain aspects of this condition violate all the classical, traditional ways that we have come to know what cities are, because they challenge definitions of cohesiveness, and are unknowable. They define a philosophical condition of uncertainty that can be read in our work. It has parallels in other urban areas like Mexico City and Tokyo, in that it is impossible ever really to know them. If you lived here your entire life, you would never completely understand this city, because it is changing more quickly than you can occupy its edges. It's a city that is almost a hundred miles across at its widest point. It is a metropolitan region, totally at odds with the normal coherence we associate with cities, as extensions of small villages of the kind still prevalent in Europe.

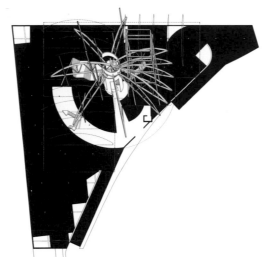 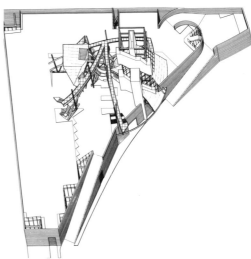

Hayden Tower
Project, Culver City, 1992
Eric Owen Moss

Petal House
West Los Angeles, 1984
Eric Owen Moss
Like the Gehry Residence,
the Petal House is both an
extension and a remake of
an existing property. The
difference is that here the new
is overlaid explicitly on the old,
in accordance with what the
architect calls the 'Stacked
House' theory: 'If there's a
roof there you don't tear the
roof out; what you do is use
the apex of that roof to locate
the new floor and then you fill
in the zone between – the
"erogenous zone". That zone
here is the studs, vertical-grain
fir and plywood, but reversed,
so that you can see the sticks
and the plywood on the outside
and you can read the
construction.'

Vienna, for example, is cohesive, and has an edge.
Los Angeles is boundaryless, with districts and
townships bleeding together into a continuous
urban map. With that comes a lack of hierarchy,
displacement of the centre into multiple centres
and a redefinition of inside and outside. Instead
of the safe inside and dangerous outside of
the past, the city today is reversed because the
inside is dangerous and the outside is safe, and
it is the American phenomenon of fleeing to the
exterior that predominates. Ultimately, this is not
about architecture, but infrastructure, flow,
movement, fluidity, lack of fixity. One factor of
the heterogeneous makeup of this culture is a
conflictual condition. Rather than representing
the harmonious place of memories ... cities today
are about radical tensions resulting from different
people trying to live together. This can be seen as a
positive condition, but also presents enormous
problems which if not confronted, create
homeostasis since there is a natural balance of
these conflicts that is reached before they become
destructive. Lack of such balance is the reason why
Los Angeles burns every 20 years or so.[8]

Global shifts in the focus of power, concurrent with
the end of the Cold War, as well as the reverberations
of the second industrial revolution in its electronic
phase, have also changed the rules of context,
increasing the frequency of interaction on a much
wider stage. As Mayne describes this factor, which
has played such an important part in establishing
his tectonic attitude: ' To me that conflictual nature
is really the essence of the modern city... The methods
by which we formulate our values are defined within
this broader framework of context. One of the
consequences of this breakdown in the notion of
community is the loss of the cohesive concept of the
public role, accompanied by a continued
advancement of the private persona, as is
characteristic in architecture today. The nature of this
series of private world views that makes up our
pluralistic world is, in my mind, one of the major
issues. One of the possibilities that grows out of this
condition is an architecture that oscillates between
these two poles, maximizing their conflictual status.'[9]

The Yuzen Car Museum on Sunset Boulevard is an
anomaly in this regard, a contextual sign for the cars
it houses, sited on a street that is symbolic of their

Lawson Westen House
Los Angeles, 1993
Eric Owen Moss
As the first major residence that Eric Owen Moss has completed since notorious examples like the Petal House type-cast him as an unpredictable practical joker, the Lawson Westen House promises to revise previous, misguided notions about his depth and capacity for complexity. Imagine a hybrid of Piranesi's Carceri and Frank Gehry's Aerospace Museum interior rendered at domestic scale, and that begins to approximate the spatial excitement Moss has achieved with this house.

iconography. Quite literally a formalized off-ramp, glorifying the cars it displays to those passing by on the cruising strip of adolescent legend, it has been designed to take advantage of a steep change in gradient, digging into the slope in order to join building and site together. Such organizational strategies may also be seen to be a consistent element throughout Morphosis' meteoric history.

As in the Indianapolis 500 race that originated in Mayne's home town, keeping a competitive edge is an important aspect at this level of endeavour, and position is everything. By interlocking figure and ground in a way that has historical precedents, but runs counter to the recent public image of architecture in Los Angeles, while simultaneously fragmenting it, Mayne continues to pre-empt the options of others, and stay ahead. This extends from general to specific, and is evident also in Mayne's attitude towards technology which, while not exclusive, is not fully conciliatory either. Where conditions make it difficult

to interlock building and landscape, as they have in the Salick Office Tower / 8201 Building or the MTV Studios, by Mayne's office, other recognizable strategies have been implemented, or negated, to create fission. In the Salick Office Tower / 8201 Building, a dialogue between old and new, of the kind evident in the 6th Street Residence, 72 Market Street and Kate Mantilini Restaurant, was not possible, leading to a decision to cut the building in two vertically, with one side facing east and the other west. The existing mechanical penthouse is sheathed in a mask which recalls the profile of Albert Frei's Aluminaire House, and stone cladding has been used as a foil against the 1960s curtain wall genre of the tower's opposite half, to arrive at the 'both-and' condition which is achieved by excavation and fragmentation elsewhere. The way edges are dealt with, as deliberately exposed, thin lines, rather than being doubled back to give substance to a point where materials change, happens too often to be

circumstantial, contributing to an overall impression of both stability and impermanence.

Morphosis remains a particularly sensitive barometer of the temper of the times in the city, based on an individualistic desire to stake out unclaimed ideological territory. In this regard Thom Mayne can be seen in the context of Sci-Arc, as well as in the city at large, to rival Eric Owen Moss, whose contribution to the MOCA Case Study programme exhibition has been discussed earlier. Moss shares studio space at Sci-Arc with Mayne and like him uses the studio as a sounding board for his own ideas, as do many others in the school; he issued his recent commission for a commercial project on the island of Ibiza as a problem for third-level graduate students to tackle. Much of the conscious dichotomy seen in Morphosis is absent from Moss's work, where the emphasis is on instinct rather than strategy, and while there are some intriguing similarities – particularly in methods of model study, presentation, and attention to detail, as well as an equally reflexive attitude towards the exterior environment – there are many significant differences. While literary allusions are also present, they are less discernible in expression.

Contrary to the intentionally temporal architectural statements made by Morphosis, Eric Moss frequently makes reference to his distrust of a conventional notion of time, the futility of seeking permanence, and his belief in the irrational need to 'keep trying'. He makes allusions to concepts such as opposition, contraction and evolution, aligning himself with Elias Canetti in a belief that architecture should seek 'nothingness only to find a way out of it and marks the road for everyone.'[10] Moss describes his platonic transformations as internal order, combined to create hybrids, such as cones which join with cylinders to make 'cocylinders'.

Heavy metal, supposedly chosen for durability, is ubiquitous in his work, adding to the star-ship metaphor so popular with Sci-Arc today. When it cannot be used, for functional or financial reasons, it is simulated, as on the skin of the Lawson Westen House, which looks like metal but is actually two shades of stucco blended by trowel. Metal is also the material of choice for models, since it gives them

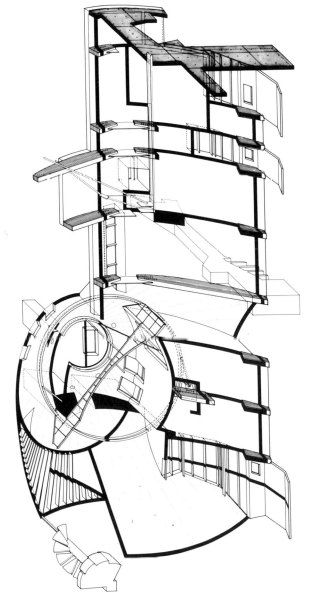

Lawson Westen House

Eric Owen Moss pays tribute to the owners of the house, who balance a love of cooking with an equal passion for collecting art. They wrote in their brief to the architect: 'Some people who collect art minimalize everything to highlight the art: white walls, innocuous carpets and furniture, minimal architectural details. We'd like to balance our art with strong architecture, colours and other details. Living in a house should be like living in a piece of art, not just living in a box you use to look at art.' Moss has done just that, realising the clients' wish for habitable sculpture, without sacrificing comfort, in one of his most skilful, and important designs to date.

Lawson Westen House
The geometric ordering of
the house is complex and
challenging, yet in Moss's
terms, explicable: 'The
cone/cylinder kitchen depends
first on the centre of a square
which is the geographic centre
of the site. The centre of the
square is also the the centre
of a circle that locates the
roof deck. The apex of the
theoretical vault is drawn
through that centre point.
A ring beam concentric to
the centre supports the cone
roof. The kitchen cylinder is
adjusted pragmatically and is
tangent to one edge of the
square. It is further elaborated
with an inscribed nonogon
map.'

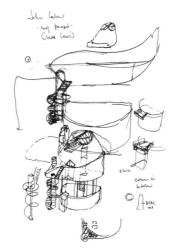

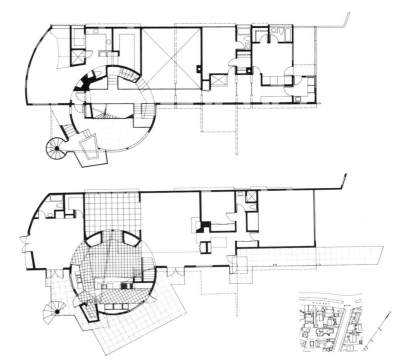

the appearance of foreboding now considered almost a prerequisite in these dangerous times. The '*Blade Runner* scenario', frequently alluded to by many writing about the city, has become a self-fulfilling prophecy that is imitated by many who share the film's nihilistic vision of an uncertain future. There is small comfort in the fact that interpretations of this uncertainty have thus far been relegated to walled compounds in Brentwood or Pacific Palisades, since the purchase by developers of the air rights over the old Western Pacific Railroad tracks has now made it possible for this extensive commentary on the city actually to become the city. Architecture that Moss has called 'a defence against nature', has suddenly become a real possibility, and on an impressive scale. His reference to Los Angeles as 'another broken city, where everything moves sometimes violently, sometimes imperceptibly either outside or in your head',[11] contradicts his claim elsewhere that the city has had no established order. In contrast to the orthogonal references to Mercator co-ordinates, as an extension of the urban grid, used by Morphosis, Moss has a visceral trust in what he calls 'emotive geometries' which are implemented to divine a new governing system where none now exists.

Through his affiliation with a developer based in Culver City, located mid-way between downtown Los Angeles and Santa Monica, Moss has had the opportunity to build complexes that incrementally connect together, such as the Paramount Laundry-Lindblade Tower-Gary Group Complex, completed between 1987 and 1990. While at first appearing to be an assemblage of separate buildings, the group eventually begins to make sense as a plaza for Los Angeles, typically built for cars instead of people, with a continuous face to the street and a gate. There are also various layers of vehicular recognition, from the orthogonal alignment with the curb on the exterior edge, to the adaptation to parking space requirements on the inside, with a final acknowledgement of the freeway, which runs by Culver City, in the distance. As Moss explains: 'The roof system of Paramount, the turned vault and the roof system of Lindblade Tower, and the turned pyramid, have an orientation to the Santa Monica

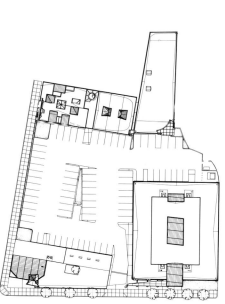

**Paramount-Lindblade-
Gary Group Complex**
Culver City, 1987-90
Eric Owen Moss
There are intriguing parallels,
and contrasts, between this
cumulative complex around the
corner from Moss's Culver City
office and the Piazza della
Signoria in Florence, even
though such a comparison may
initially seem to be somewhat
far-fetched. Each piece in the
development is the result of
growth by accretion, taking a
matter of years in California,
and centuries in Florence.
Each has also been prompted
by motives related to influence
and commerce, with defensive
architectural gestures in this
case pointing to local unrest.

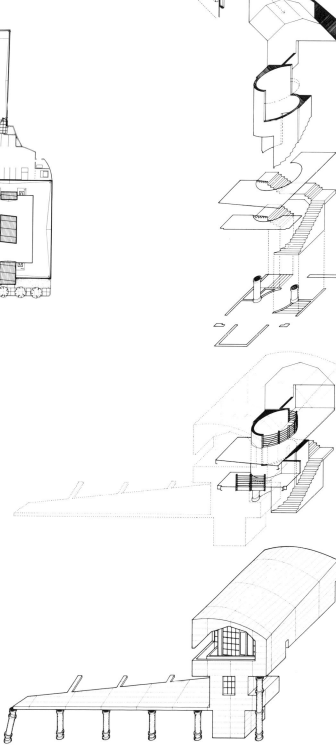

Freeway. The roof sensibility is therefore not to the
order of the city streets, which the elemental building
blocks themselves acknowledge.'[12] This use of a
personal language to describe or interpret a collective
order is the point of tension for Moss, generating the
binary oppositions he is always dealing with – of
public and private, known and unknown, resolved
and unresolved, making and disassembling – resulting
in what he half-jokingly calls a 'Penelope theory' of
architecture. For him, however, the 'ravelling and
unravelling' he refers to has to do with his search for
an elusive urban logic, and the eventual imposition
of another, mental equivalent that arises in the wake
of the frustration of not finding one. This kind of
invention is quite distinct from, on the one hand, the
approach of Frank Gehry as evinced by the Loyola
Law School where he reconstructs the Acropolis on
Olympic Avenue within an isolating high steel fence,
and on the other hand from the attitude of
Morphosis, whose new Los Angeles Unified School
interpolates between the street and the landscape:
Moss's invention has more to do with trying to
comprehend the incomprehensible. A Babylonian
map of the sky, which is a favourite analogy that the
architect uses, could just as easily be replaced by a
sixteenth-century map of the Earth, since there are
extreme inaccuracies in each, and although our
knowledge of both sky and earth has since improved
immensely, he emphasizes that cartography is still an
inexact science. In his own charting of the past to
determine which way to go at present, and in the
future, Moss stresses his reliance on personal
judgement, and interpretation of his own version
of reality, since no collective consensus exists. Seeing
such creative schizophrenia as 'a cure and not a
disease', this architect looks for durability in things
that are constantly changing, and seeks to re-invent
things he has already invented. There are generic, if
not specific, historic references to be found, such as
the tortured campanile and clay-pipe arcade of the
Lindblade Tower, which looks vaguely Italianate
in rusticated block.

The Gary Group, on the other hand, is admittedly
Mayan, with its slanted ballcourt wall and machinery
superimposed as a technological update, indicating

Paramount-Lindblade-Gary Group Complex

As Moss says of the complex's central open space, 'this is the typical Los Angeles quadrangle - a parking lot'. If parallels can be drawn between Florentine and Los Angeles models, this space can also be seen to underscore the priorities of each age since the traditional piazza was obviously intended for its citizens; here, that role is inverted. There are presently three completed buildings on the site, and a fourth is planned. Thus far it has successfully redefined a rundown area of Culver City which Moss describes as a 'nowhere place', giving to it an element of durability and stability.

Paramount-Lindblade-Gary Group Complex

The Lindblade Tower is the closest that Culver City may ever get to having a Palazzo Vecchio, and yet, while the absence of civic space continues to be an interactive problem in Los Angeles, Moss, and other architects who insist that the public realm is illusory are possibly more accurate in their assessment of the nature of the contemporary city. The resulting protected interior environments, or 'Cities Within' as Frank Israel refers to them, are the result of sophisticated electronics, civil uncertainty, and many other factors, but are now a fact of life in LA which nostalgia seems unable to reverse.

a prolonged fascination with the Yucatán.[13] The western wall around the corner, facing the parking lot, extends the mechanical metaphor, with chains draped across it and with its reinforcing bar ladders, like so many zippers in vertical lines spaced at regular intervals across the elevation. Ivy planted in the boxes beneath is intended eventually to grow on the ladders, which will give the entire façade the appearance of an exotic ruin, rusting away in the sun. This uninhibited 'visual hedonism', as Moss calls it, corresponds to a now familiar approach to the by-products of technology, and to the general consensus that it has made a somewhat flawed contribution to society. A delight in the tactile sensuality of the parts here is balanced by an evident distrust of machines in general, since the pulleys don't pull and the chains don't move, implying a more complex symbolic agenda as well.

The majority of Moss's work is speculative office space, for undetermined tenants, who will almost certainly be replaced by many others throughout the lifetime of the building. His reaction to change not only relates to a shifting cityscape, but to uncertainty of use, in marked contradiction to the Modernist dictum of 'form follows function'. Form, then, is as speculative as the venture itself, generated out of an educated guess, always to be reconsidered. Once functionalist prerequisites are discarded, similar principles – of structural honesty and showing things as they are – must also be questioned, as must the myth of off-the-shelf prefabricated industrial components which was raised to the level of orthodoxy in James Stirling's Leicester Engineering and Cambridge History Faculty Buildings back in the 1960s. The fact behind that myth, which Moss has turned into a virtue on its own, is that the manipulation and customization which high technology inevitably requires, once embraced rather than denied, allows the freedom to personalize without restriction. The phenomenal thing about the majority of Moss's work is that such freedom, not normally permitted by most financially motivated

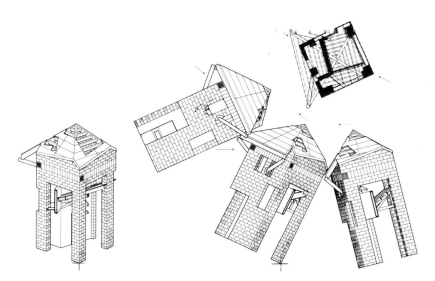

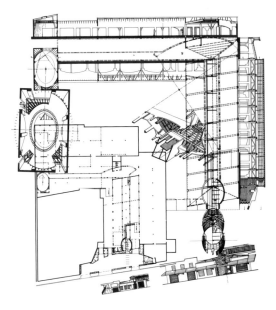

Conference Room
8522 National Boulevard
Culver City, 1988-90
Eric Owen Moss

As the centrepiece of five light industrial buildings that have been refitted to house a variety of clients, the conference room at 8522 National Boulevard concentrates many of Eric Owen Moss's preoccupations into a single space that remains one of his most memorable. Lined in birch plywood, which is cut away in certain places around the elliptical outline of the room to expose concrete block or wooden stud-work, the conference space has an other-worldly quality that comes as a complete surprise after the linear experience of dappled light and shade typical of the sky-lit offices and central public walkway leading to it. With characteristic perversity, and humour, Eric Owen Moss has taken great pains, to show clearly what is old and new, by strategically placing gaps in the conference room's lining where they can be most easily seen, allowing a deliberate peek behind the scenes carefully arranged for his audience by the 'producer' of the show. In spite of the obvious, stage-like character of the skin, however, the magical thing that Moss achieves is a suspension of disbelief through this candour – which is quite different from the intentional visual disjunctures that Frank Gehry sets up using similar materials.

developers, has been encouraged by an enlightened patron who not only understands that it sells space, but who takes a wider view of the general improvement of the territory in which he has chosen to operate. Such collaboration, although not exclusive here, is certainly rare.

When client and function are known, and speculation is not a factor, as in the Lawson Westen House on the UCLA side of Sunset Strip, completed in 1993, the degree of invention is even more complex, because of specificity. The programme here dictated a professional kitchen for a couple who cook together and entertain frequently. The vertical funnel above the food preparation area that results, like the kitchens of the Topkapi palace by Sinan, is a dominant form, all the more so because it is monolithic, its roof undifferentiated from the vertical side wall except by a thin, curvilinear line that swirls along the side of the cone. Sketch studies for this element reveal the mental gymnastics of a contemporary geometer in action, and serve as a reminder of why this title was synonymous with that of architect in the Middle Ages, even though it has since been forgotten in the loose mathematical requirements of many schools today. Moss accepts as an a priori truth that one purpose of architecture is to contrast human with natural order, giving less emphasis to the second part of that pairing. As he has said: 'At some level, every project involves a kind of manipulation or transformation of what's given, either literally, or figuratively, or both. What I don't want to do, is give you back something that is monochromatic, single-minded (somehow single-minded and simple-minded are close to each other) so that if something is simply symmetrical, or simply balanced, or simply linear, or simply a narrative, then it's simple-minded. My experience of the world is not that.'[14] The Piranesian world described inside the cone of the Lawson Westen house, which puts the fantastic spatial explorations of Lebbeus Woods for example into practice, is incomprehensible at a single glance, and only partially revealed in ascent, through compositional vignettes accumulated on the way up a series of separated stairs. The effect is exhilarating and mentally exhausting at the same time since, as Moss says: 'The solution of a difficult quadratic

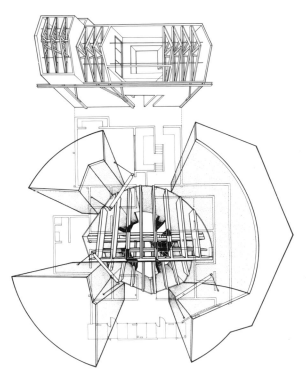

Goalen Group
8522 National Boulevard
Culver City, 1988-90
Eric Owen Moss
Moss's strategy for the Goalen
Group is similar to that for the
neighbouring Qualitative
Research Center; the plan is
organized around a central
focal event which in this case
is the screening room, Goalen
being a film maker. This space
is focal in the sense that, 'it's
the place that everybody goes
through on the way to doing
whatever they do.' It has
consequently become known
as the 'street corner' although
it is more accurately an
intersection in plan. The
vertical elements defining this
space are projected upward
through the roof-light, cutting
through he clerestory
sawtooth and leaning inward
as they rise, indicating the
force of the deformation that
has been made in the existing
fabric.

equation is absorbing and yet taxes the brain.'[15]
Throughout the copious sketches that are used to
evolve those geometries, scribbled literary references
show they are not peripheral to this process, and not
quoted only for effect. An equal number of pragmatic
notes about plumbing and mechanical systems, which
balance these, also indicate points of co-existence
and transition from unbuilt to built form.

In the Arnodt House, different, but equally
complex equations have been employed in a more
literal statement of the precarious point between
stability and disequilibrium. This ball-like building,
with various segments cut out in a progression of
interrelated volumetric surgeries, is tentatively
perched on the side of its cliff-side site, deliberately
posing the same kind of questions about the order
that it suggests just as the Lawson Westen house does.
The Arnodt House, which extends the circular great
hall of the Lawson Westen House into three
dimensions, steps into previously uncharted territory,
both spatially and structurally, since it is not only
even more difficult to comprehend, but is also
constructed entirely of brick. This imaginative
recycling of ideas from plan in one instance to section

in the next, from the central zone in an early house
to a conference room much later, or just in details that
later emerge as entire rooms, is a characteristic shared
by other architects in this city, who begin to construct
a formal language as experience permits and
consciously rework previously unrealized thoughts
at different scales. In this instance, due to the amount
of work now completed, and the high probability that
opportunities to build will increase, such invention
promises to provide excitement in a continuing
re-mapping of the city for some time to come.

The strong connection between Morphosis, Eric
Owen Moss and Coop Himmelblau, another practice
with a Sci-Arc power base, is illustrative of the global
compression of influence today and the insignificance
of distance to these architects, who jet off to attend a
birthday party in another country at a moment's
notice. Wolf Prix of Coop Himmelblau, who is a
visiting critic at Sci-Arc and has collaborated with
Thom Mayne in the formulation of the Los Angeles
Arts Park project, is a significant, if sporadic presence
in the city, and represents a departure from others in
the Sci-Arc axis because he has led Coop Himmelblau
into an involvement in planning issues as well. Their

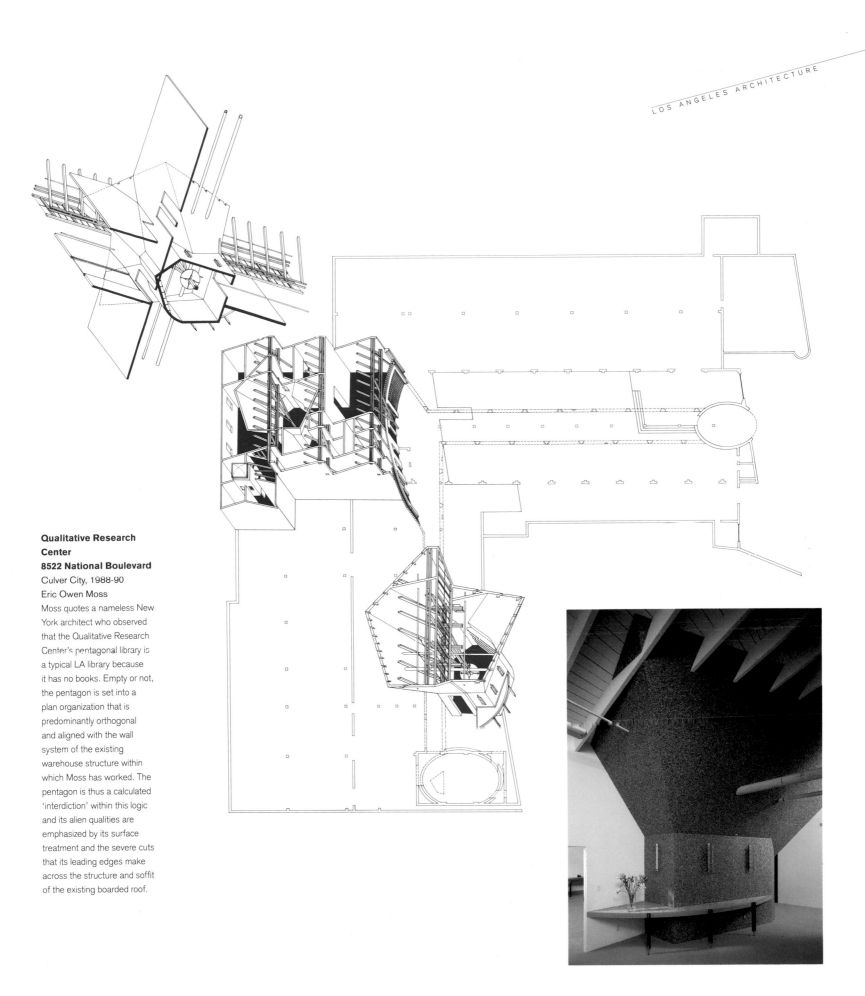

Qualitative Research Center
8522 National Boulevard
Culver City, 1988-90
Eric Owen Moss

Moss quotes a nameless New York architect who observed that the Qualitative Research Center's pentagonal library is a typical LA library because it has no books. Empty or not, the pentagon is set into a plan organization that is predominantly orthogonal and aligned with the wall system of the existing warehouse structure within which Moss has worked. The pentagon is thus a calculated 'interdiction' within this logic and its alien qualities are emphasized by its surface treatment and the severe cuts that its leading edges make across the structure and soffit of the existing boarded roof.

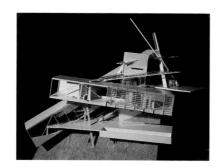

Rehak House
Project, 1993
Coop Himmelblau
Unlike the Open House, which began as a non-specific frenzied stream of consciousnes, the Rehak House was designed with a Los Angeles client and site in mind, which makes the distinct similarities between the two even more difficult to explain. But, in these days when architects travel everywhere, why can't a building or individual styles? A major project that Coop Himmelblau originally designed for Fukuoka, Japan, was moved to Sapporo, and another work now in design in Los Angeles itself has moving parts; both seem to be appropriate conditions for a firm that has always sought to embrace the ephemeral. The prospect that Coop Himmelblau may eventually build more in LA is in itself exciting.

work to date, aside from the Ewe Mess Station in Weis, Mariahilfer Platz in Vienna and Europaplatz Centre in St Pölten, Austria, has mostly been at the residential or office conversion level in Los Angeles, however, and their projected Open House in Malibu, continues themes seen in earlier work. As a defiant rejection of theory, the design, which has been adapted from an earlier, siteless experiment, is an instructive polygraph, first drawn like braille, with eyes closed. It is expressed as half tent and half glass pavilion, with the addition of over-scaled venetian blinds made necessary by the Californian sun. As an intentional translation of Karl Popper's *Open Society and its Enemies*, the pavilion, with a fractured transparency that is as illustrative of the principles of Deconstructivism as Philip Johnson's iconic Glass House in New Caanan, Connecticut, was of those of Modernism before it, will require an equally strong ego to occupy it.[16] The pylons required by local code, pinning the flat platform on which the building sits on to its steep hillside site, have made the translation

from an ideogram in Vienna to the actual sunspace of California quite painless, but the louvres and the angular bracing that they require have made the spontaneity of the original diagram disappear beneath vertical stripes.

The strong opposition to theory expressed by Wolf Prix, who is not as ready to make literary references as are his friends, is an anomaly in this axis, and all the more noteworthy because of the extremity of the architecture he produces. For all of its disjunction, it also demonstrates the same concern for detail and precision seen elsewhere among the Sci-Arc group. As Prix has said: 'We, Himmelblau, have no theory [and are] very proud of that fact... if we split theory from building, I think the same will happen to architecture. We see more and more virtual reality, and it is not by chance that architecture now – and I can read it in the work of the students – is becoming an escape from reality, and I think one of the hopes of theory could be that it bring reality back into built space.'[17]

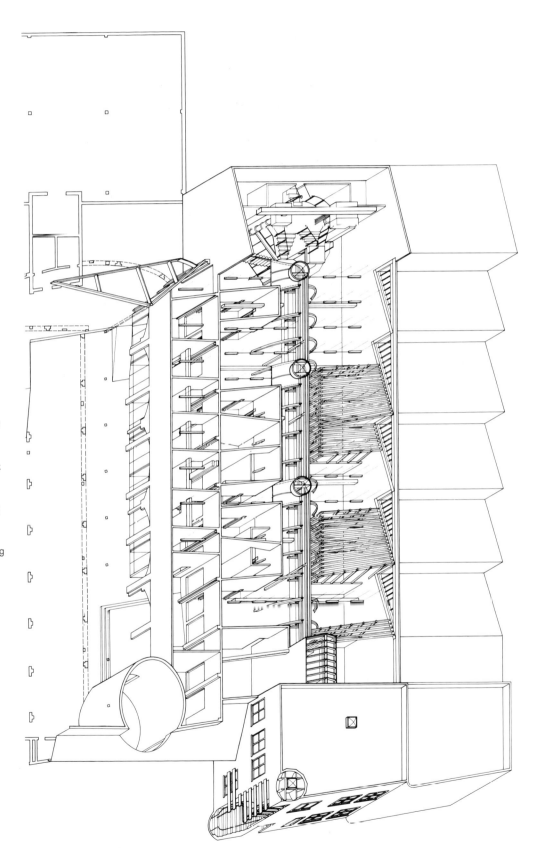

Scott Mednick Offices
8522 National Boulevard
Culver City, 1988-90
Eric Owen Moss

The offices for Scott Mednick
Associates are formed from
the parts of four pre-existing
structures. Here, the unifying
gesture is a large central
hallway which is lined with
workstations on one of its long
sides. Spatially, this element
is defined by a line of semi-
circular ribs which are
suspended from a roof beam
that forms a new centre line
and datum in the plan. In
Moss' words, 'all of the ribs
are the same but amended
in terms of how they are
supported or what they
intersect.' One rib goes
through a wall and comes
out the other side; some
are sawn off to avoid wall
to beam collisions and
others are either propped or
deformed to connote special
events in the plan.

Saee House
Los Angeles, 1991
Michele Saee

Michele Saee perhaps more
than any of the latest
generation of architects in the
Sci-Arc axis, personifies the
slick-chic approach to
materials that may be
discerned as a trait in the
school. He has managed,
however through a novel
approach to form and
juxtaposition of unlikely
elements, demonstrated here
in his own house, to carve out
a signature style in a city
where achieving a design
identity is particularly difficult.

If the Open House represents this version
of reality, it does so at the level of structure and
connective tissue, rather than as a platform from
which to view the Pacific (only seen through slits and
slices), or as an energy-conscious passive solar house,
since it requires an air-conditioning plant as large as
the building itself to keep it cool during the summer.
Coop Himmelblau's Rehak House, on the other hand,
differentiates between city and ocean view, and is
configured as an 'X' in order to accommodate each,
as well as the land form on which it is built. Since it
was designed for its site, rather than imposed on it,
the house may be seen as a revision of the Open
House, or what the latter would have been had the
site been known beforehand.

In spite of the deceptive frivolity of such
confections, Coop Himmelblau, as evidenced by their
earlier 'Flaming Wing' exercises, have sprung from
more anarchic tendencies than either Morphosis or
Eric Moss, but all three share an inveterate urban
phobia, and Coop Himmelblau's decree that 'tough
times demand tough architecture'[18] is certainly one
upon which they all agree.

Of the other, more visible members of the axis in
no particular order of priority, Michele Saee has also
established a reputation for fine detailing, mostly
through his own house and a series of elegant
commercial interiors, which have included the Angeli
and Angeli Mare restaurants, several clothing shops,
and a dental surgery in Beverly Hills. Experience in
the film industry, in the design of sets for the
Terminator series by Paramount, have expanded
his range and place him solidly within the Sci-Arc
firmament, in spite of the relatively small scale of
work completed to date. His penchant, as an alumni
of Morphosis as well, is for fine craftsmanship, an
incongruous mix of materials, with a characteristic
soft spot for metal, and an ironic attitude toward
technology, all blended together in a minimalist
and unmistakably personal style. Retro-fitting is an
inevitable part of the niche that Saee has carved out
for himself as Los Angeles' futuristic answer to Adolf
Loos, whose Kärtner Bar hides behind a pre-existing,
anonymous exterior offering few clues to the jewel-
like detail within. In his transformation of a dental

Saee House

Characteristically, Saee's work indulges in the interplay between the tactile and visual qualities of different materials, as a means of highlighting their physical essence rather than being polemical. In the residence he designed for himself, the sensitivity that Saee has become known for is finally evident on a large scale; and if there is a stylistic debt to be recognized, it is obviously not to Morphosis or others in the Sci-Arc axis, but rather to the 1930s, the heyday of Hollywood, when elegance and panache were appreciated. Rather than deliberately adopting the architectural language of that period, however, Saee has shown that he instinctively understands its spirit.

surgery, 'treatment pods' are screened off from the main reception space by highly polished wooden shields, connected to the roof by matt black metal standards which also channel electrical power to the drills mounted behind them. Aneline green flooring, in contrast to the rich brown screen, provides an effective and inexpensive means of delineation between the waiting room and the chairs, where the flooring changes to sleek black tiles. As in his other installations, the combined effect of this quirky palette of materials is of a refined aesthetic unusual in a city best known for temporary construction, which in its own quiet way, is helping to change this image.

Craig Hodgetts and Hsin-Ming Fung, of MOCA Case Study fame, are doing the same in recent projects such as the temporary quarters for the Powell Library, or 'Towell', that they have provided for UCLA while the original undergoes renovation to meet seismic codes for public safety. Although now affiliated mainly with the University of Southern California at San Diego, Hodgetts and Fung retain visiting critic status at Sci-Arc, where they have taught since 1987, with offices within walking distance of the old studio in Berkeley Street.

The Gagosian Gallery, realized in collaboration with Robert Mangurian (who is the director of the graduate programme at the school and principal of Studio Works, to which Hodgetts was affiliated from 1969 until 1984), as well as recent projects such as the Thames Residence in Los Angeles, displays similar concerns of craftsmanship and fine detailing, making it a recognizably consistent product of Sci-Arc axial planning.

The stiff competition for commissions mentioned earlier, especially in what now appears to be a permanently readjusted economy, has meant that paper and exhibition architecture now make up a large part of aspirants' portfolios, serving as a creative outlet and means of refining theoretical positions. Never, it would seem, have such daunting reputations been established on so little built work. For some, such as Lebbeus Woods, this has remained the medium of choice, and has had wider repercussions than the work of many practitioners with a long list of projects to their credit. Like Piranesi, whose spatial visions have had an enduring influence that has transcended cultural and historical boundaries, Woods has through his consummate graphic skills

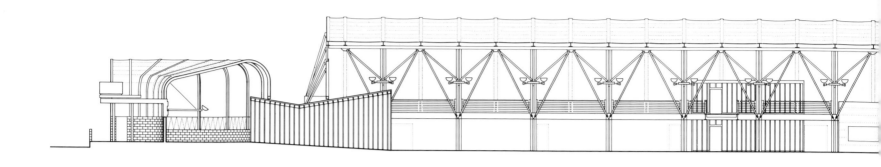

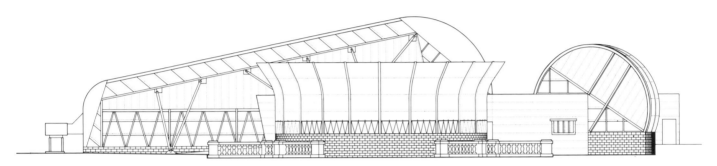

Temporary Powell Library
Westwood Campus UCLA,
1992
Hodgetts & Fung

The temporary home of the
Powell Library, or 'Towell',
houses the main university
collection while the existing
building is refitted to meet
more stringent seismic codes.
The imaginative product of
expediency and a restricted
budget, it is built of readily
available industrial parts, and
meant to be disassembled
after three years. The Towell
is designed to respond to,
rather than exclude, the
exterior environment. Passive
rather than artificial climate
controls are used to maintain
the interior temperature at the
levels necessary for protection
of the collection and for user
comfort.

been able to capture the imagination of many, and
is particularly popular among students who identify
with his inspired, illustrative images, free of
gravitational restrictions. As the Hugh Ferris of the
1990s, Woods prescribes a 'heterarchy' that is just as
free of previous human associations, rising through
each city to establish new hierarchies, social
groupings and typologies. While not specifically
related to Los Angeles, the harsh, mechanistic visions
that he creates strike a responsive chord with
students, who see similar attributes of the city in
them. In his Aerial Paris, Terra Nova, Underground
Berlin and Zagreb Free Zone projects of 1988 to
1991, the specific location has been less critical than
the ideas proposed, all revolving around the familiar
article of faith that the individual, rather than the
group, is the paramount arbiter of reality. In Woods'
opinion, 'individuals, not communities and societies,
are the highest and most complete embodiment of the
human', and 'only in the field of sensate, sensual
experience – the field embraced by the idea of
architecture and the city – [can] self-contradictory
attempts to understand the state of the human find
their common, exalted basis.'[19] His Centricity project

of 1987, which involves a network of cities each with
an autonomous centre, comes closest to describing
Los Angeles, driven as it is by 'fluidity, indeterminacy
and dynamic equilibrium in an urban field'.[20]

Such a love of graphic 'non physicality', as Thom
Mayne puts it, may also be seen to be alive and well
in the work of Paul Lubowicki and Susan Lanier,
graduates of Sci-Arc who have worked for Frank
Gehry and Morphosis respectively. Their reliance,
however, moves away from science fiction to the
wacky world of Krazy Kat cartoons, which is an
equally selective version of reality. Their O'Neill
Guest House in West Los Angeles embodies the
bunker mentality now endemic there, in spite of
retaining a playful use of a marine metaphor with
its rowboats, oars, and a bridge over the pool.
Immediate recollections of Frank Gehry's Camp Good
Times, the House for a Film Maker and similar
whimsies, come to mind in this embankment, which
is both childlike and serious, and drawn as being
much more frivolous than it actually is.

Reliance on the graphic image, or the growing
trend toward 'non-physicality', is a fertile theme in
analyzing the Sci-Arc axis, and carries on into the

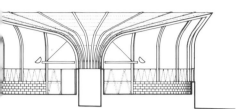

Temporary Powell Library

The 'Towell' was completed in six months, at a cost of just under $3 million, and is now cited as a possible prototypical solution to the problem of homelessness in Los Angeles, and as the basis for structures to replace those burned down in the cyclical 'uprisings'. The temporary facility is popular with faculty and students alike, to the extent that reservations for its limited carrel space are as difficult to come by as a well-positioned table at Spago. When, and if, it is dismantled, the Towell is certain to achieve that mythic level hitherto occupied by more physically substantial structures.

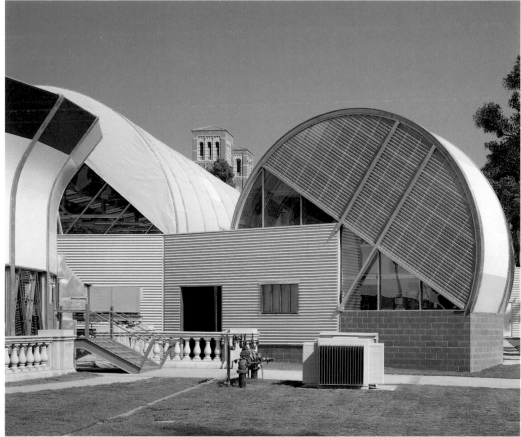

Domore Showroom
West Hollywood, 1986
Hodgetts & Fung
One of the smallest projects
completed by this firm, the
Domore Showroom was
designed for an office furniture
company, as part of
Westweek, held annually in the
Pacific Design Center, nearby.
This event, attracts a global
contingent of architects and
interior designers, and Domore
wanted their display to be
incorporated into their own
headquarters. Craig Hodgetts
and Ming Fung proposed a
billboard to be integrated with
the outside of the building,
which would be visible from
the front door of the Design
Center itself. The result is
described by Ming Fung as
'an invitation card in 3-D'.

O'Neill Guest House
Project, West Los Angeles, 1992
Lubowicki Lanier

The Gagosian Gallery
Venice, 1980
Craig Hodgetts with
Robert Mangurian
Located near the 72 Market
Street Restaurant by
Morphosis, the Gagosian
Gallery is miniscule. Although
the gallery, like 72 Market, is
ancient history in a city where
Andy Warhol's concept of 15
minutes of fame is taken
seriously, the Gagosian's
circular courtyard has become
an icon of sorts because it, like
Los Angeles, was invented out
of nothing, and uses glitz and
gloss to distract attention from
the hard reality around it.

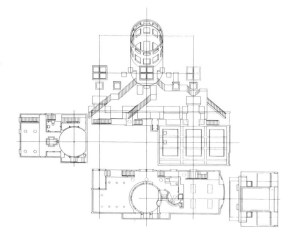

Brix Restaurant
Venice, 1991
Central Office of Architecture
With principles that are all
aligned with the Sci-Arc axis,
and some of whom are alumni
of the Morphosis office, it
should be no surprise that the
Central Office of Architecture
approach their work with a
similar emphasis on process.
A drive-through health-food
restaurant, Brix occupies a site
surrounded by highly chaotic
commercial fabric. The new
building consequently presents
itself as a billboard in the
tradition of Frank Gehry's
Santa Monica Place, forming
a recognizable street elevation
to potential customers as
they drive by at relatively
high speed.

murky world of competitions as well. The probability
of a competition having enough impetus and public
relations appeal to propel an obscure young firm into
the public eye is highly unlikely, but when this does
occur, as it has with Zaha Hadid and the Peak
Competition in Hong Kong, or with Maya Lin and
the Vietnam Memorial in Washington, the
architectural media are particularly responsible for
perpetuating or burying the aspirants. Hani Rashid
and Lise Ann Couture, who met while attending
Carlton University in Canada, have since formed
Asymptote, named after a mathematical term
meaning 'to bring diverse things together'. Their 1988
entry into the Los Angeles Gateway Competition
organized by Nick Patsaouras, and its subsequent first
prize, has increased their visibility dramatically. The
paradoxically titled 'Steel Cloud' that they submitted
– a metallic, deconstructed freeway for people instead
of cars – won in the face of formidable opposition
because it fulfils several layers of civic expectation all
at once. California's answer to the Statue of Liberty,
the Steel Cloud signifies that Los Angeles is now the
Ellis Island of the 1990s: just as Vladimir Tatlin, in his
Monument to the Third International, reconfigured
the Eiffel Tower (designed by the engineer of the
Statue of Liberty), Rashid and Couture have
deconstructed the lady with the torch to signal a new
social, rather than socialist, order. Its present, supine
position recognizes that most immigrants now arrive
on four wheels, or by aeroplane, rather than by boat,
which is where its second point of appeal lies.
Proposals for bridging over the freeway have recently
become quite numerous, as part of the current 'unite
LA' syndrome, but few have had much merit or
inspiration. The Steel Cloud, which traverses eight
lanes in a single bound, quite literally elevates the
humdrum typology of pedestrian bridge to new
heights, as a matrix for walking over the unfortunate
souls below. Bow-string arches, also of steel, which
seem to be a deconstructive prerequisite among the
axis (as can be seen in the Morphosis scheme for the
Los Angeles Arts Park) makes this big leap possible,
and adds a bridge-like sign. The only negative note
is an emphasis on electronic billboards, to include
the car-bound populace in the action as well. This

Brix Restaurant

Occupying a typical 100-foot-wide commercial lot, Brix sits behind a long floating screen wall placed between the street edge and the face of the building behind. This semi-transparent mask, constructed of perforated metal and a variety of steel sections, operates as both a filter, dampening the visual and audio noise generated by the street, and as a 'found urban object' pulled from its normative functional context, to amplify the presence of the restaurant on the site.

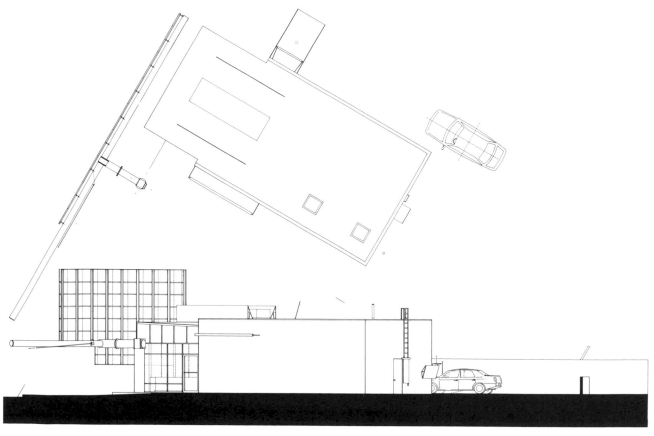

Steel Cloud
Los Angeles West Coast
Gateway, Project, 1988
Hani Rashid and Lise Anne
Couture: Asymptote
The Steel Cloud is a metallic
deconstructed freeway
intended for people instead of
cars. As California's answer to
the Statue of Liberty, the Steel
Cloud announces the fact that
Los Angeles is the Ellis Island
of the 1990s and as such it
appears suitably psychotic. Its
tangled web spans eight lanes
of traffic elevating the
fortunate pedestrian above the
miserable incoming masses
trapped in the jams below.

supposes, of course, that in the midst of watching
out for bandits at 6, 9, and 12 o'clock, as well as for
police in unmarked cars ahead and behind and in
helicopters above, people have both the time and
ability to read about the Dodgers' latest double play.
This insistence on including the media, however,
possibly stems from a belief that no symbol of this city
would be complete without it, and is also congruent
with Asymptote's recent experiments in optigraphics.

At the opposite end of the technographic scale,
Nader Khalili, the charismatic author of *Racing Alone*
who runs a special graduate programme in vernacular
architecture at Sci-Arc, may at first seem like an
incongruous blip along the leading edge. However,
the 'hands on' approach that he takes in his course,
as well as in the apprenticeships he offers in the
community he is building in Hisperia outside Los
Angeles, are in keeping with the overall philosophy
of the school, and his work has generated a great deal
of interest. He has updated Hassan Fathy's techniques
of building in mud brick by using ceramic glazing
techniques that permit a soluble material, which
would otherwise be unsuitable in the torrential rains
of this area, to become feasible. He is also working on
prefabrication techniques for brick vaults, bringing
the technological questions raised at Sci-Arc full circle
to address an age-old construction method.

This brief overview of the activities of only a
few of the Sci-Arc staff gives an indication of the
institute's diversity and influence, both locally and
internationally. The interesting thing in the near
future will be to see to what extent that position can
be sustained, and if it will grow, as a bellwether of
the stance that it has come to represent among one
segment in the city. The discussion that follows is
of another equally influential, if less strident faction,
with a diametrically opposed agenda, which has
managed to stake out the unclaimed ideological turf
of community values and the relationship between
these and architectural typologies. Geographically
close to Sci-Arc, but light years away ideologically,
UCLA, under the leadership of well-known urbanist
Richard Weinstein, presents a compelling case for the
importance of connectedness, evident in the work of
a cadre of adherents throughout the city.

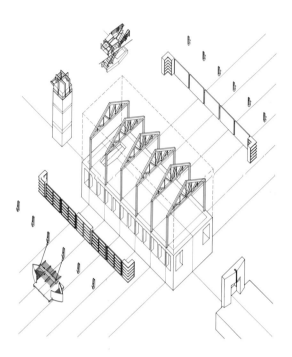

Architecture and Community: Divining a Sense of Place

Unlike those architects that have either a theoretical or pragmatic affiliation with Sci Arc, those in the UCLA orbit do not have an identifiably similar style, but seem to share an interest in historical precedent and a belief in the importance of a connection between architecture and the various communities throughout the region. In recognizing this difference, the academic allegiances of the major participants discussed here at least begin to provide one framework for establishing boundaries, and one that can lead to a degree of understanding about what is happening in the city at the moment.

Franklin Israel, for example, who teaches at UCLA, acknowledges his influences in a refreshingly straightforward way. Having come from the east coast of the United States, he attended the University of Pennsylvania while the Philadelphia School led by Louis Kahn was at the height of its power there. He also attended Yale and Columbia universities, followed by an extended residence at the American Academy in Rome where, like Robert Venturi, he concentrated on Renaissance and Baroque history. Israel has drawn from this experience, incorporating it into his work and giving it a broader base. While he

Art Pavilion
Beverly Hills, 1991
Franklin D Israel
Designed to contain a gallery
for the client's large art
collection, this pavilion also
contains two floors of studio
space. The eight-acre site on
which it is located slopes down
to a stream and a dense
eucalyptus grove, which the
architect has made into a
terraced sculpture garden.
The pavilion has been
conceived as a piece of art
in this garden, rising up like
a great Ark containing a
precious cargo of Abstract
Expressionist paintings. Grand
stairways and an outdoor
loggia, as well as large corner
windows establish a direct
connection with the site.

reiterates the prevailing sentiment that each architect
in Los Angeles should be considered as an individual,
outside of Gehry's shadow, he hastens to add that
when he first arrived on the west coast in the late
1970s, his first instinct had been to learn all that he
could about the city from the master. Israel alone
seems frequently to allude to the 'Los Angeles School'
with the implication that Gehry's relevance in the city
is similar to Kahn's in Philadelphia, and that there is
a discernable group who have been affected by him.
From Gehry, Israel acknowledges having assimilated
critical perceptions about the difference between Los
Angeles and other American and European cities,
particularly with regard to its being dynamic rather
than static, with colliding juxtapositions that generate
a psychological and visual energy found nowhere else
in the world. A brief but significant time spent in the
special effects department of Robert Abel films made
Israel's conversion to Los Angeles architect complete,
and yet the formal strains of European Modernism,
filtered through the historical and geometrical screen
so intricately fabricated by Kahn, are all evident in his
work, which is where he parts company with the rest.

Because of this background on the east coast Israel
has been more able to identify two separate
geometries in Los Angeles, which have informed his
architecture. The grid, as the first of these, is usually
not recognized because freeways now overshadow it,
making surface streets mentally invisible, and yet
Israel, who comes from New York City with a fresh,
perceptive eye, feels its force. Because of his early film
connections, he has received many commissions for
studios and record company offices, which are
frequently located within this framework and where
work schedules are typically not restricted to an
eight- or nine-hour day and often go on runs of days
at a time. Consequently, his designs of those
complexes become urban anagrams, or 'cities within'
as he calls them, with streets and houses, public
spaces and gardens laid out in a grid tied to exterior
co-ordinates. Israel's residences, on the other hand,
are mostly situated in the hills, which 'violate' the
grid and introduce the need to distinguish between
architecture and landscape, in order to define what
the purpose of building is.

Israel strongly believes that this dialogue between
the built and the unbuilt is what makes Los Angeles
different. His emphasis on the recognition of two
systems, and the need to respond differently to each,
may seem elementary, and yet has rarely been clearly
stated elsewhere, as the confusion over expression in
such a bifurcated context prevails. Israel echoes Philip
Johnson in his belief that Los Angeles is at once 'the
ugliest city in the world' and located in the most
beautiful physical circumstances imaginable, which is
certain to result in tectonic schizophrenia.[1] Drawing
parallels between Los Angeles and Japan – which
Israel identifies as playing the same role that Rome
did for the Philadelphia School, as a psychological
and formal paradigm – Israel notes that there are
similar contradictions of scale and centres of energy
that exist here, but that they occur with greater
frequency and at a higher magnitude than in Tokyo.
The Pacific Rim and the California Coast, which is
its mirror image, is the contemporary equivalent of
Socrates' Frog Pond, around which the Greeks once
sat, calling out to each other across the Aegean. Asia
Minor, as the eastern edge of that circle, frequently
surpassed its western alter ego in flashes of creativity
and new discoveries, and yet the western component
has prevailed because of persistence, consistency and
duration. The strong economic influences which the
Japanese have exerted in Los Angeles are now
waning, but the drawing power of the culture is
strong and continues to grow.

It is fascinating to note that a reverence for
Japanese architecture – as expressed by Greene and
Greene, and their ultimate homage to it in the
Gamble House; by Frank Lloyd Wright, who began
his interpretations of the Ho-o-den Temple at the
Columbian Exposition of 1893 with the Prairie Style,
and evolved it further in his Los Angeles houses; and
by Rudolph Schindler in the Kings Road House,
which had such an impact on the Case Study houses
that followed – has been perpetuated by Frank Gehry,
Thom Mayne, Eric Moss, Frank Israel and Moore
Ruble Yudell, among others, irrespective of academic
base. The stress (at Sci-Arc in particular) on
craftsmanship in general as well as on specific
disciplines such as Sumi-i, is a continuation of that

Art Pavilion

Israel's pavilion has windows which use mitred glass corners reminiscent of those employed by Wright and Schindler. These windows also prescribe rhythmic breaks in the interior, where art cannot be hung. The gallery is a 28-foot-high space framed by large timber trusses. Moveable walls allow it to become a reception or lecture space as required, with regulated natural light. The architectural focus of the space is an open stair linking this upper, main gallery with the spaces below. Materials are fibreglass reinforced concrete walls with glass panels set in mahogany frames, with stucco also used in certain areas to match the existing house next door. The roof is of sheet metal and custom-made tile, with accentuated scuppers.

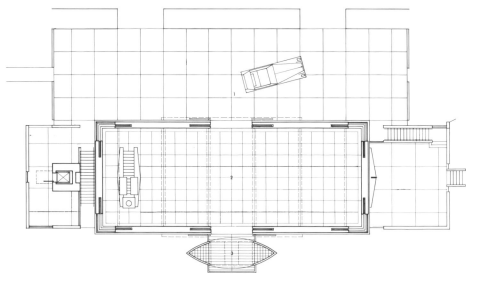

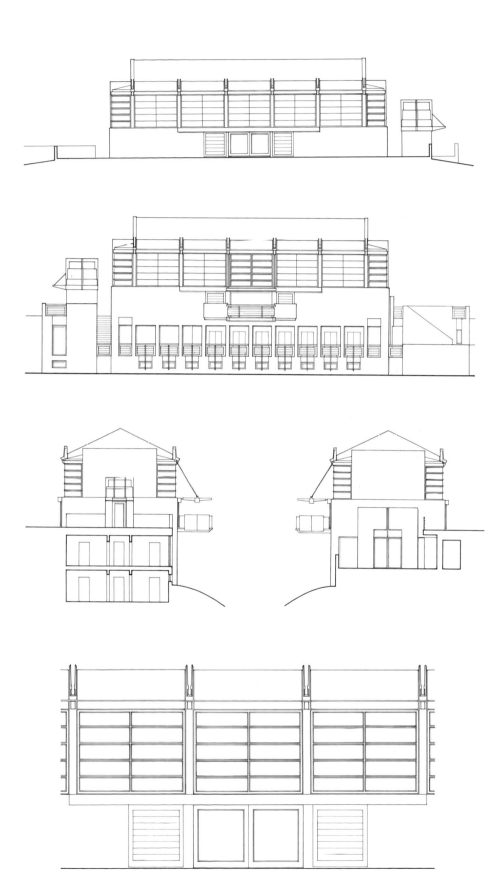

tradition, even if stylistic connections are now more difficult to trace. The economic stake that Japan holds in Los Angeles, as well as the sheer numbers of Japanese-Americans that live there, reinforces this connection, as does the belief among many Los Angeles architects that they, and their Japanese counterparts (especially in Tokyo) are steps ahead in terms of experimentation with their new and radically different ideas in architecture, especially involving computer aided design.

Two of Israel's most recent projects offer specific examples of his highly individual approach to the classic problem of defining territory between building and site. His Art Pavilion, in Beverly Hills, which includes a gallery for the client's extensive art collection as well as two floors of studio and related spaces, had to conform both to a steep slope and to the large home situated next door, to which Israel looked to provide clues for his own direction. Specific elements such as staircases, terraces and loggias are used to join house and site, as are large corner windows, which the architect has employed to frame carefully selected views of trees and sky, deliberately perpetuating what Israel describes as 'the tradition started in Los Angeles by Wright and Schindler of the mitred glass corner and the exploded box. These windows prescribe rhythmic breaks in the interior where art cannot be hung.'[2] The top floor of the pavilion is a gallery with a 28-foot-high ceiling framed with timber trusses. A seemingly weightless stair joins this to another gallery below it, as well as to a smaller photography gallery, archive, guest quarters and laboratory. An underground passage connects this great 'Ark', filled with Abstract Expressionist art, to the existing house next door. The materials used are reinforced concrete and glass in mahogany frames on the upper level, with stucco used below to tie it to its neighbour. A boat-shaped balcony reinforces the 'Ark' concept, and its delicate covering of wisteria and bougainvillea make it seem that a sculpture in the garden below has levitated and become connected to the gallery wall.

The Raznik House in the Hollywood Hills, on the other hand, has a somewhat more conventional programme, with the addition of a guest apartment,

157

Virgin Records

Beverly Hills, 1991

Franklin D Israel

As with Israel's Limelight Productions, the Virgin Records project involved the remodelling of an existing structure. Because of the wide diversification of interests within the company, the offices required a great deal of subdivision. The physical separation of corporate divisions led to an almost symmetrical arrangement of the interior. A T-shaped, axial pathway serves as a datum, lined with private offices. At the intersection of the crossbar and stem of the 'T', a cylindrical amphitheatre creates a third zone of interior space. The idea of reductive sculpting, implied by the carving out of the T-shaped path from the office grid, is carried over into the seating of the amphitheatre, which appears to be cut from a solid curved wall.

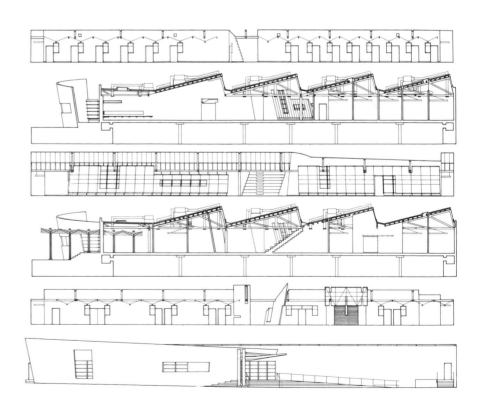

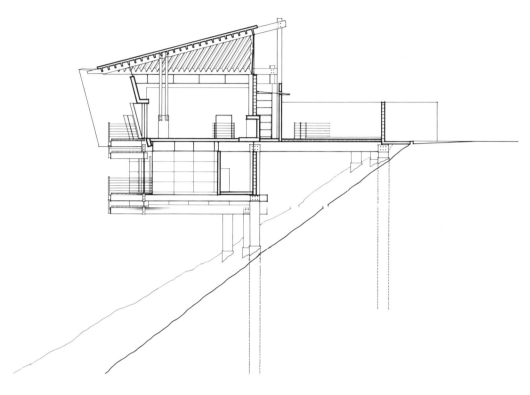

Raznik House

Project, Hollywood Hills

1991

Franklin D Israel

Frank Israel frequently refers to the unusual topographical conditions in Los Angeles, and the Raznik House intentionally recalls the best traditions of hillside architecture in the city. The nadir of the heavily wooded canyon in which the house is located, has been used as the centre of an arc which extends to form a curved structure that echoes the dramatic landforms of the hillside. Raising this structure has allowed vegetation to continue to grow up the hillside, and among the piers which lift up the house, emphasizing what the architect has called 'the fifth façade'. Along the street, the concave form of the house creates an exception to the anonymous wall that is so common along the curving roads of the Hollywood Hills.

which Israel has located above a garage, using a stair tower for access. This tower, in turn, becomes the major vertical feature of the design, visually anchoring its curvilinear form to the hillside in a way that is deliberately artificial, thus distinguishing it from the wildness of the canyon below. As Israel says: 'Los Angeles is still largely defined by its topography and the distinctive vernacular of its various neighbourhoods. The Raznik House seeks to reinforce this strong sense of context by shaping itself to its dramatic site, as well as recalling, through its vocabulary, the exciting history of hillside architecture, from Neutra to Lautner, of which it is a part.'[3] The structure of the house is an extension of the concrete pilings driven down into the hillside as a foundation, with wooden 'glu-lam' beams spanning the columns. The curved elevations are treated as thin screens of plaster and glass, while the roof is metal. Interior walls run parallel to this screen, and are made of wood frame, glass and steel.

Lest one should think that these parallels of individual reference and natural association, constantly reiterated by Israel, are superficial, it should be pointed out that the rationale behind them

has been a direct reaction to Los Angeles, to which the architect constantly refers. That rationale explains Los Angeles as a place of margins rather than centres, one which began as a background for the fabrication of myth, and has now been made introspective out of fear. The subsequent separation from reality – the world outside – has occurred, in Israel's opinion, because of traffic, smog and violence, and he feels that architects must sympathize with a client's negative response to all of these. He draws unexpected analogies between this city and Rome, which he also knows well, citing their original founding in relationship to topographical features as the most obvious similarity between them. Beyond that, he uses the invented word 'dialogical', which implies both dialogue and place, in order to define a feeling of mental projection induced by both, of not being where you are, but where you want to be. He attributes this to many things, including pre-existing alter egos which have acted as urban mirrors against which each city has tried to formulate an identity. New York, which has served this purpose for Los Angeles as Athens did for Rome, has held the title of the cosmopolitan, cultural capital of the United States

159

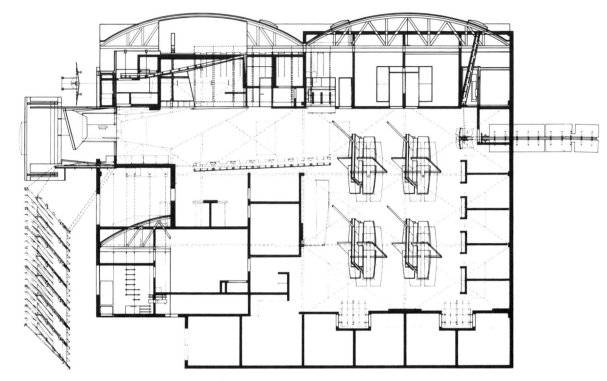

Limelight Productions
Hollywood, 1991
Franklin D Israel
The Limelight Productions
project involved the
remodelling of a large
warehouse space, roofed by
bow-string trusses, distributed
along two matching bays.
These, as well as a small site
and limited budget, established
strict parameters for the
design, and suggested the
careful articulation of an
entrance sequence, beginning
at the western wall and
continuing on through the
entire length of the interior.
Fenestration is used to call out
the main entrance, and once
inside, canted walls and
skylights help to emphasize
the movement pattern through
the space. Individual offices
are organized according to the
established pattern of the roof
trusses, with each work station
treated like a 'sculptural
grouping'.

for the entire lifetime of the nation, and has
traditionally been the emotionally charged gateway
to it, until Los Angeles usurped that position during
the last decade. Most tellingly, Israel sees both Los
Angeles and Rome as sources for the dissemination of
popular culture, throughout an empire in the earlier
instance, and across the globe at the moment. As he
has said: 'One could as easily paint a comparison [of
both] in terms of diffusion, diversity and decadence.
Certainly both cities must be framed as crossroads as
well as destinations. If "all roads lead to Rome", as
many roads must now depart from Los Angeles. On
the distant fringes of their respective continents,
Rome and Los Angeles are both final outposts of a
dominant order and first havens to the newly
enfranchised; whether in the forms of bath houses
and amusement parks, or in the figures of Caligula
and Bret Easton Ellis, the two cities have periodically
redefined luxury and dissolution as few locales have.'4
These comparisons refer to the concept of a selective
individual vision of reality in regard to a particular
city, based on experiences which may or may not be
relevant at the present time, so that the city becomes
a state of mind more than an actual place. This

interesting idea is certainly true in relation to Los
Angeles. While every city goes on changing, these
visions colour our relationship to those we feel we
know well, making objective observation difficult.
This love of cities, and the subjective baggage of
memory connected with it, visibly transfers into
Israel's work, particularly in his commercial projects
which become 'internal villages', complete with
microcosmic renditions of each civic element used in
the larger model, allowing him to provide the sense
of human scale and closure that he feels Los Angeles
lacks. Limelight Productions and Virgin Records,
as two of the latest of these projects, point out this
transfer in different ways.

The Virgin Records offices, as an example of
Israel's notion of 'interiority', have taken a number
of forms. The initial project was to be located next to
Gehry's Chiat Day in Venice, but the client finally
decided on a site in Beverly Hills which required the
interior and exterior remodelling of a 28,000-square-
foot warehouse. Virgin, as a recording company with
diverse interests, required a greater subdivision of
office space. A corporate division between the
business and creative offices led to a plan that is

**Goldberg Bean
Residence**

Hollywood Hills, 1992
Franklin D Israel
Perhaps because he is a
relative newcomer to a city in
which almost everyone can
trace their roots to somewhere
else, Frank Israel has been
more openly receptive to
topographic imperatives and
historical precedents than
many others, and will gladly
identify them. His ability to
synthesize several local
vocabularies into an expressive
personal style, while adding
unexpected twists of his own,
is particularly evident in the
Goldberg Bean Residence,
an extension and remake
of an undistinguished 1950s
bungalow in the outpost
section of the hills. Israel
added a foyer/gallery and
a master bedroom tower and
reclad the original structure to
create a much more expanded
but unified composition.

Goldberg Bean Residence

The Goldberg Bean Residence illustrates Israel's broad frame of reference, whereby specific features, borrowed from the best examples of the Modern Movement, are combined with his own, distinctive approach to the site and client brief. He cites the MOCA 'Blueprints for Modern Living' exhibition as a bench-mark in this regard, and the influence of the Case Study prototype, where interior and exterior spaces flow freely into one another, is evident in the planning of this house. Israel's objective readings of the past also provide helpful clues to the continuing viability of certain stylistic directions in the region today, which can be seen to be alive and well in his work.

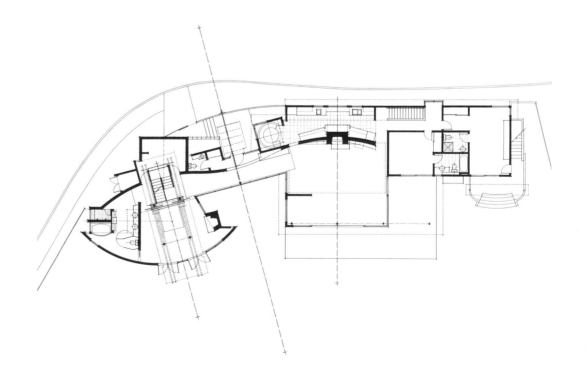

almost symmetrical, resulting in an axial scheme that
is more direct than that of any other project he has
done before. Here, most circulation paths are lined
with private offices and the grid of closed spaces came
to serve as a datum defining the 'negative' space of a
a T-shaped pathway.

At the intersection of the 'T', a solid cylindrical
amphitheatre presents a third zone of space within the
interior. As the paths were carved from the office grid,
the stairs and stepped seating of the amphitheatre
were conceived as reductive sculpting. They appear
to be cut from a solid round of material, serving both
as seating and as circulation space. As Israel has said:
'Following the earlier designs for the Venice site, the
exterior plays subtly on the name and nature of
Virgin. A low "V" marks the entrance to the
headquarters, and a long curving outer wall presses
out toward the street. The billowing curve recalls the
"hulls" of previous work and coyly suggests that
Virgin may be more "pregnant" with inspiration than
its name would indicate. Though no longer affronted
by the multivalent architectural machismo of the site
on Main Street in Venice, the Virgin complex in
Beverly Hills fends off the cool advances of her
neighbours with graceful composure.'[5]

The project for Limelight Productions involved
remodelling a large double-bay warehouse space in
Hollywood. As with a similar project for Propaganda
Films, the space is defined by a series of bow-string
trusses aligned along two evenly matched bays.
A compact site and limited budget set many of the
parameters for the commission, indicating that much
of the design focus be placed on the articulation of an
entry sequence, beginning outside the building's
western wall and continuing through the entire length
of the interior. A twisted sun-shade, adapted from
Le Corbusier's Villa Stein, creates an enforced
perspective, pointing out the entrance to the offices.
Inside, a canted wall becomes an extended low
canopy that defines the reception area, while a back-
lit, translucent, fibreglass surface, shaped like a shield,
completes the eastern end of the axis. A free-standing
wall has been used to baffle the light of this corridor,
fragmenting glare from the skylight above. Individual
offices follow the established pattern of the ceiling

trusses, surrounding a group of assistants' workstations. Here, composite desk arrangements, patterned after those used by Frank Lloyd Wright in the Larkin Building and the Johnson Wax Headquarters, are used as sculptural elements to symbolize the new administrative organization being used by the company.

Conference rooms and public spaces are concentrated near the entrance to create the impression that the complex is much larger than it actually is. The elegance of the entrance arcade, combined with the expanded scale of the assistants' stations, is intended to imply a large multimedia corporation, rather than revealing what a modestly sized company Limelight actually is. Materials and details are consistent with this approach, with rich, birch plywood used in all cabinetry. The edges of all laminated materials are exposed, to show their real substance; aluminium fasteners, joints, wall bases, hardware and sheeting are introduced to raise these

items above utilitarian connotation. Glass and fibreglass complete the palette, balancing transparency with opaque surfaces. The selection of materials and colours used by Israel have proven to be very effective, with the tactile collage of brick, wood, aluminum, glass and fibreglass reinforcing one another in surprising ways.[6]

Demonstrating similar sensibilities, albeit in a somewhat different formal vocabulary, the office of Moore Ruble Yudell is also decidedly outside the Sci-Arc orbit. This firm, which has proven to be extremely successful since first designing the Rodes House, completed in 1981, accurately reflects the urban design emphasis instituted by UCLA dean Richard Weinstein, who is a product of the Louis Kahn studio and has worked as a city planner in New York City. While completed under the aegis of the Urban Innovations Group rather than Moore Ruble Yudell, the Beverly Hills Civic Center is a good example of Moore's continual search for a proper

Rodes House

Los Angeles, 1981
Moore Ruble Yudell
Designed for a bachelor professor who wanted a serene formal retreat, the house evolved from the limitations of cost and topography. Due to unstable land fill, the house spans its hillside site using a buried bridge of caissons and grade beams. A lightweight lattice structure behind the house's curved façade recalls an earlier proposal to place the trusses within the exterior walls. As a distant echo of Wright's Olive Hill, an oval patio serves as a stage for performers visiting the client's university while guests sit in an orange grove that contains fragments of a terraced amphitheatre.

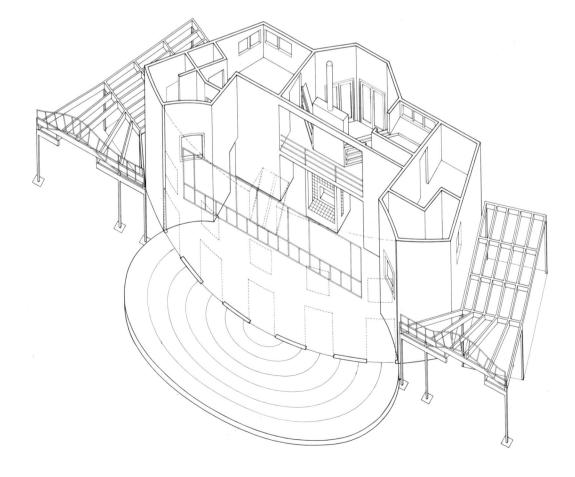

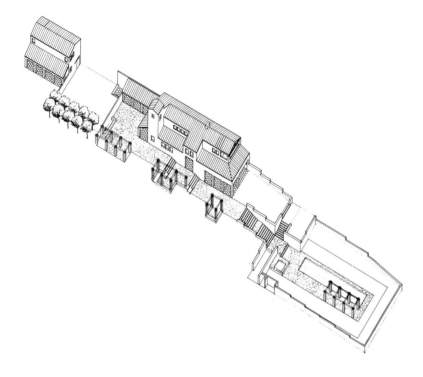

Yudell Beebe House
Malibu, 1991
Moore Ruble Yudell
Built for architect Buzz Yudell and his landscape designer wife Tina Beebe, the house evolved from the constraints and virtues of the site. From east to west the residence is defined as a series of progressively less formal layers of inhabitation: from conventionally organized rooms for living and sleeping, to a sun lit gallery large enough for seating and dining, to a stepping terrace and pergolas that delineate outside 'rooms' of varying character, on further through cultivated gardens and finally to the wild chaparral beyond.

setting for the *res publica*, if such a thing exists in Los Angeles, as best expressed in his article 'You Have to Pay for the Public Life', which is contemporaneous with Robert Venturi's *Complexity and Contradiction in Architecture*.[7] The competition-winning design, which presents a formal face to Santa Monica Boulevard to the north and only reveals itself fully when entered from a monumental stair to the south, is based on a sequence of landscaped courtyards that connect a remodelled City Hall, new fire station and police headquarters, and public library, with partially submerged parking structures that seem like landscaped terraces when seen from the street. For more than a half-century, the spire of the City Hall around which the project revolves has been the symbol of Beverly Hills, and the entire complex of new or renovated buildings is intended to extend its visual reach rather than isolate it. Accordingly, the height of the new buildings has been aligned with the base of the tower and one of these wings has been extended to bridge over Rexford Drive; the rhythm of the bays used also replicates those of the City Hall.

A major axis, running diagonally past the City Hall, joins three elliptical courtyards. These are ringed by rows of palm trees, followed by arcades that front the buildings and support a series of ramped walkways that facilitate shared access between the various departments. This diagonal sequence suggests a natural progression from the downtown area of Beverly Hills, through a monumental gateway, and into the gardens; this device has been used by Moore Ruble Yudell in many projects since, as a more subtle means of interconnection, and to encourage the use of the landscaped spine. A recent residential project in Kobe, Japan, is after Beverly Hills the most direct example of this approach to date, showing once again that many of the city's major firms, regardless of affiliation, creed, or lack of either, have strong connections across the Pacific which affect their work in either overt or subliminal ways.

Plaza las Fuentes in Pasadena, a project which imposed even more restrictions on the architects than did the Beverly Hills Civic Center, also relates to a historic City Hall, just across the street. Because of property line positions, and an existing church, the curvilinear tactics of Rodeo Drive had to be restrained, and a rectilinear, 'L'-shaped plaza used instead. It is partially paved and partially green,

Beverly Hills Civic Center
Beverly Hills, 1988-89
Moore Ruble Yudell / Urban
Innovations Group
Built in several phases over
a three-year period, Moore
Ruble Yudell's competition-
winning scheme creates a
coherently urban sequence of
three eliptical courtyards that
connect a remodelled City
Hall, a new fire and police
headquarters, a public library
and new parking garage. The
City Hall has been a well-loved
landmark in Beverly Hills for
more than 50 years. The new
buildings take character cues
from it, both stylistically and
compositionally, and reinforce
its central position within the
development.

171

Beverly Hills Civic Center
The new buildings align
deliberately with the wings
of the City Hall, one of which
is extended to bridge over
Rexford Drive, linking old and
new structures in a direct way.
The rhythmic bay system of
the art deco City Hall is also
recalled in the façades of
the new buildings, whose
construction employs repetitive
precast concrete elements
coloured and detailed to
harmonize with the original
composition.

connecting the lobby of a major hotel and office building with the governmental complex nearby, in a carefully calculated sequence that uses fountains and landscaping to modulate scale and texture. Colourfully glazed ceramic tiles are used on all of the vertical faces of the fountains lining the linear open court, with similarly tiled panels of varying height used as a backdrop to accentuate this splash of colour. Alongside, the street's enormous arches – echoing Frank Lloyd Wright's Morris Store in San Francisco – form a continuous arcade that reduces the massing of the hotel and office portion of the grouping, giving the street level over to pedestrians. The recent renaissance of the older part of Pasadena, where Plaza las Fuentes is situated, has ensured that its open spaces will be active, making the Plaza an integral part of a downtown that can comfortably be identified as a civic success story in a more traditional sense. The project will also act as an important case study in any future discussions about the architectural ingredients that may be necessary in the ongoing search for 'place' now underway in Los Angeles. Plazas of the conventional historical variety, as an imported concept, have hitherto been problematic because of

over-reliance on the car, inadequate attention to amenities, and malls that disregard climate and fear of going out after dark. However, several well-known exceptions, such as Olvera Street and the 3rd Street Promenade in Santa Monica, have encouraged others to keep trying, with gratifying results such as this as the outcome.

Moore Ruble Yudell have also been involved with a consortium of architects in developing Playa Vista. This is a proposed mixed-use community intended to occupy nearly 1000 acres extending inland from the Pacific, adjacent to Westchester, Playa del Rey, Venice, Marina del Rey and Mar Vista, and located on land purchased by Howard Hughes in the early 1940s for aircraft testing and manufacturing. The size of the property and its strategic location soon led property developers to speculate on its potential for exploitation, and since the 1970s a number of master plans have been put forward. The rising interest in the property over the years has been accompanied by increasing concern over its impact on the region, which culminated in the 1987 election of Councillor Ruth Galanter, who ran a 'Stop Playa Vista' campaign. Her surprising defeat of the incumbent

City Council President underscored community interest in the issue of the future growth of the Los Angeles Basin.

Maguire Thomas Partners became the General Managing Partner for the Playa Vista Project early in 1989. Their initial discussions with the Council Office made it clear that the project would have no support unless the master plan was altered in conformance with community concerns in a replanning programme carried out under the closest public scrutiny. Maguire Thomas met with the community groups that had opposed previous plans, prior to beginning a design of their own. Numerous, frequently contradictory, points of discussion were raised in each of these meetings, but there was consensus on four fundamental issues: the amount of traffic that such a development would generate, the environmental threat that it might pose to the Ballona Wetlands, the conflict in building heights allowed by existing zoning (which permitted 240-foot-high towers adjacent to

the Westchester Bluffs which are only 140 feet high) and the impact on waste management and already strained water resources. Maguire Thomas then assembled a master planning team of architects, landscape architects, urban planners, engineers and other specialists chosen especially for their innovative approach to such problems, and their demonstrated willingness to work with community groups. The major members of that initial team, in alphabetical order, were Andres Duaney and Elizabeth Plater-Zyberk, Legorreta Arquitectos, Moore Ruble Yudell and Moule & Polyzoides. An inter-disciplinary workshop approach, which is a methodology familiar to each of these firms and a significantly alien concept to those in the Sci-Arc axis, was adopted as the most effective way of dealing with such a complex project, one which involves overlapping City, County, State and Federal jurisdictions and constantly changing environmental regulations. These workshops brought all parties with a stake in the project together in one

Hollywood Entertainment Museum
Project, Hollywood, 1993
Moore Ruble Yudell
This new museum will chronicle the history of the broadcast medias in Hollywood. The project involves the preservation of the 2700-seat Warner Theater which at the time of its opening in 1927 was the largest movie palace in the city.

Beverly Hills Civic Center
A major organizational axis, running diagonally past the City Hall, provides a spine for three eliptical courtyards, each ringed by rows of palm trees. From these courts, arcades in front of the major buildings support a series of ramped walkways that provide easy access between the various functions.

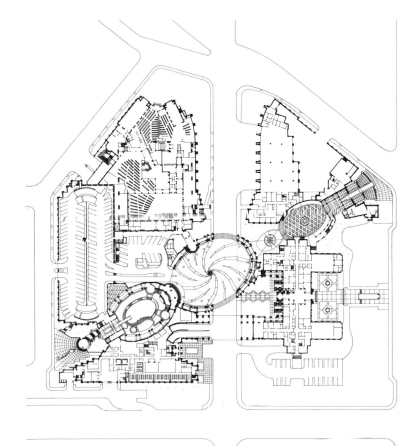

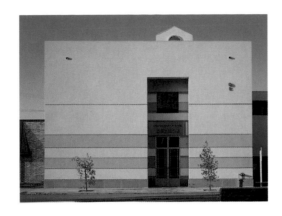

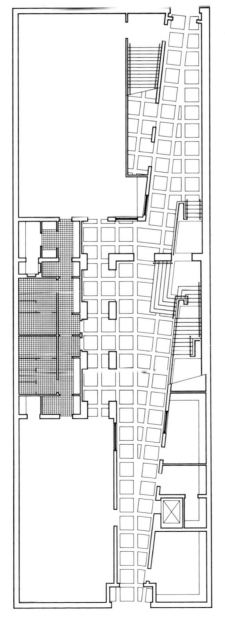

Crossroads School
Santa Monica, 1989
Moore Ruble Yudell

Known officially as the Peter Boxenbaum Arts Education Center, this part of the Crossroads School, which is a progressive secondary school located in an industrial area of Santa Monica, resulted from the conversion of a simple, concrete warehouse building. As a continuation of a private pedestrian street running throught the campus, the school's internal plaza is brought to life by the students moving through it, or using the monumental stair at its centre to reach classrooms above. Dance, art and music studios have balconies overlooking the internal street, and a second-floor gallery can be opened up, allowing the entire population of the school to become participants in a changing daily performance.

place over a concentrated period of time in order to determine a clear planning direction.

The master plan that finally emerged from this series of workshops is markedly different from those that preceded it, in several significant ways. Firstly, it puts forward a revision of the segregated approach to zoning typically seen in the past, introducing the concept of mixed use on the site. The final proposal has decreased office use by nearly one million square feet, retail space for regional use by nearly half a million square feet, and hotel space by 1350 rooms, and in contrast to existing zoning, which permits buildings of twenty stories or more, it prohibits buildings taller than the Westchester Bluffs adjacent to the site. By contrast, housing has increased by more than 4000 units, concentrating on multi-family rather than detached accommodation, showing the extent to which Maguire Thomas has invested in the idea that people are now willing to forego the elusive delights of suburbia to live in a self-sufficient, mixed-use community, where commuting will not be necessary. The success of this model in several other instances, such as a mixed commercial-residential block in Santa Monica built recently by the Janss Development Corporation, shows that this bet may not be as risky as it seems in a city that has grown weary of demarcation, isolation, and the freeway, and where people moving in from other urban areas all over the world are demanding the convenience, and vitality, that comes from proximity. The implication of such a mix amidst increasing heterogeneity is nothing less than the creation of a new social model here, and a paradigm for the future. Indeed precedents for it, mostly dating from before the post-war dependence on the automobile which made suburbia possible, do exist in Los Angeles, where densities of 20 to 30 dwelling units per acre were once common.

The second significant outcome of the community workshops, as reflected in the Maguire Thomas master plan, was a determination by the developer to resolve a lawsuit by the Friends of the Ballona Wetlands against the previous project sponsor which challenged the legitimacy of land use determinations affecting this environmentally sensitive area. To do so, the untouched area of the Wetlands was increased by

First Church of Christ Scientist
Glendale, 1989
Moore Ruble Yudell
Continuing a line of Los Angeles community churches that includes St Matthew's Episcopal Church in Pacific Palisades, the First Church of Christ Scientist in Glendale draws together two small congregations. The plan is centred on a courtyard facing the street, from which the main auditorium, Sunday school buildings, offices and meeting rooms are entered. The auditorium foyer is placed at the front of the site, forming a glassy bay that draws the movement of the courtyard into the building and, in the evening, creates a glowing pavilion of light along the street.

50 acres, and $10 million has been set aside to restore and maintain it, which has allowed the long standing lawsuit to be settled. The basic premise of the master plan is that a more carefully balanced mix of land uses, in a low-rise configuration, with a street system primarily designed for internal rather than regional use, can generate a strong sense of community without placing any appreciable burden on the infrastructure around it, and that its design can encourage self-sufficiency.

Because of their background in analyzing historical residential prototypes in the region, Moule & Polyzoides, as participants in the initial design consortium of Playa Vista, have been particularly aware of the typological options that exist, and have been working with landscape architects Hanna/Olin on a fascinating study of how these types combine with indigenous trees to form several characteristic street configurations. These configurations have then been utilized in various parts of the Playa Vista plan, depending on the scale and width required, going beyond simple formal translation in establishing verified, pre-existing regional connections.[8]

The Playa Vista master plan is best described as a series of neighbourhoods, organized according to a uniform set of planning principles, which are intended to function individually and yet coalesce through transportation and open space networks. Residential blocks have been used as the fundamental unit of Playa Vista, and the plan calls for a wide variety of them. Each is based on the premise of proximity between living, working and shopping, so as to be self-sufficient. Streets, parks, civic and cultural buildings, ground floor retail and office uses and residences form the principal parts of each neighbourhood. Residential buildings are designed to be low-rise and multi-family, arranged in such a way as to define, rather than be defined by, the streets between them. Courtyards and internal gardens are used extensively, continuing the hierarchy of open space, from large to small, implied by the overall plan. The grouping of retail outlets along a 'transit spine' ensures that daily shopping needs can be served in the neighbourhood, without residents having to drive great distances. Up to 50,000 square feet has also

Plaza las Fuentes
Pasadena, 1992
Moore Ruble Yudell
This mixed-use development,
on a six-acre site in the heart
of the historic district of
Pasadena, includes office and
retail space, hotel and
conference facilities and public
gardens, organized in such a
way as to reinforce the City
Hall nearby as a civic landmark
and a focus of urban activity,
as it was intended to be in the
original city masterplan. A
series of carefully designed
courts links the promenade
and gardens of the Plaza to
the City Hall and the existing
street pattern around it, with
the 360-room hotel serving to
anchor the pedestrian street,
or 'paseo', at its opposite end.

been set aside for small businesses along this spine.
A grid has been used to provide both visual and
vehicular continuity from outside the site boundary,
and yet the street has been approached differently,
as an appropriately scaled 'traffic path' which also
encourages pedestrian use along tree-lined sidewalks,
rather than the slim concrete ribbons that are now
the rule.

In describing the approach that Moore Ruble
Yudell take in their work, of which their extensive
involvement in the Playa Vista project is only one
part, Buzz Yudell dismisses stereotypes related to a
particular style, and the idea of a set manifesto, and
refers instead to implicit principles or common traits
that guide the office. Using the analogy of a jazz
ensemble, he describes improvisational structures that
help each member of the partnership, and the firm in
general, to contribute. The first of these is the need for
collaboration, which is usually seen elsewhere as a
threat to creativity or a diminution of a strong
concept, but is regarded by this group as a pleasurable
exercise that extends upwards from a team in the
office, to the client, and the community at large.
Countering the myth of architect as genius seen
elsewhere in the city, and the idea of architecture as
a unitary act of will, Moore Ruble Yudell substitute
a faith in shared values, and a belief in the evolution
of a concept through group discussion. The second
principle they all share is the need to discover in each
instance the underlying logic of each problem,
including the *genius loci* and 'territory', as Mario
Botta calls it, which goes beyond legal surveys, as
well as an indelible order. This last, which involves
geometry, is in their view often not pure or overt, in
a rational sense, but does relate to set theory,
contingency, and experience relative to function and
use. These, when pushed further, towards lines of
tension between various systems, are distorted, to
display a more accurate diagram of topography and
movement, like the overlapping force diagrams
produced by Charles Eames. Movement, which in
their public and private projects frequently begins as
the classic Beaux-Arts *marche*, typically starts to be
eroded as the order is distorted by contingency. Their
building for the Crossroads School, in Santa Monica,

is a clear example of this. The process is felt to be
experimental, rather than diagrammatic; narrative,
and not dogmatic, with steps that are subjective as
well as objective, and as such are untraceable.

A third principle is the necessity of humanism,
and the recognition of real, rather than abstract, time
and space. The Kobe project in Japan is an example
of this, relating both to its place and to a wider
framework. 'There is a tendency at the moment,'
Yudell explains, 'to downplay Post-modernism,
which is now seen as pastiche, and a cheap stage-set
architecture that has thrived through ransacking
history. There is a real need, however, to maintain
and restore the Humanistic tradition that is now
under siege in this post-Post-modern era. Charles
Moore and Robert Venturi did manage to reconnect
us to this tradition, to successful historical examples,
and not just shapes, as well as timeless ways of
dwelling, human aspirations, and sensations. In the
more than 7000 years that architecture has existed,
there are commonalities that can be identified, such as
our need to feel connected to the earth, and to share
the experience of the public realm.'[9] For Moore Ruble
Yudell, the revival of Humanism today – under
whatever label – still involves these things, and they
search for ways of making buildings that confront
essential questions, in simple and quiet ways. They
differ from pure European Rationalism in that purity
and austerity are not part of their ideal, but they share
a belief in clarity of purpose and process. They part
company from the Sci-Arc axis in their inclination
to draw on context, and to use it to create tension
between inside and outside.

This quality of what Charles Moore has called the
'geode', which is rough on the outside and wild on the
inside, is now best seen in projects of large urban
scale, such as Plaza Las Fuentes in Pasadena, in which
there exists order and chaos, a distinct outside and
inside, and a sense of the passionate attempt to make
a habitable place that is served by a geometric
structure, rather than confined by it. Chance, which
may be seen to be another principle in their work,
plays a part in this, not in the free existential sense
of for instance I-Ching or the music of John Cage, but
in the discovery of process within structure, and the

Plaza las Fuentes

Pasadena city officials required the architects to reinforce a connection with the local tradition of Mediterranean architecture, and arched arcades, deeply inset openings, stucco walls and tile walls serve to make that historical connection, without it becoming a literal statement. At night, the fountains bordering the paseo reflect onto the high walls around them, transforming the gardens into a magical place that seems far removed from the the often grim urban reality of Los Angeles.

freedom this can offer in design, rather than following the rules of a linear methodology. This approach also includes a resistance to being categorized, and a freedom to use many different kinds of sources, whether they be Beaux-Arts, New Rational, De Stijl, New Expressionism or Japanese architecture. This last, however, interests Moore Ruble Yudell a great deal because of an innate ordering system, mingling of indoor and outdoor space, and lack of boundaries.

A last principle, which Playa Vista in particular represents, is to encourage a sense of community wherever possible. According to Yudell, their question to themselves in this project was: 'How can we establish such a sense in a new town?'. Their answer was as follows: 'We began by looking back at what has worked in Southern California, as well as at early Modernist failures at the urban scale, in which a *tabula rasa* approach was used that sanitized or erased parts of cities completely. Public life is encouraged at Playa Vista, and essential typologies, such as streets and

parks are refined to do that. The armature here is the idea of mixed used and synthesis.'[10]

In contrast to Sci-Arc, or UCLA, the University of Southern California (USC), as the third major architectural school in the city, is less easily categorized. After a decade of leadership by Robert Harris (ending in 1992), the school has entered a transitional period, making it difficult to position ideologically. This is especially true because of the various interests of its faculty, which makes an overall design philosophy impossible to pinpoint at present. A review of selected projects by members of staff who are engaged in architectural practice may serve to underline this diversity, as these run the gamut from the restoration of a Mission Style mansion to the design of farm workers' housing, and are indicative of the many different agenda that are legible throughout the school.

A recently completed house by Cigolle Coleman, for example, was seen by the architect owners as a

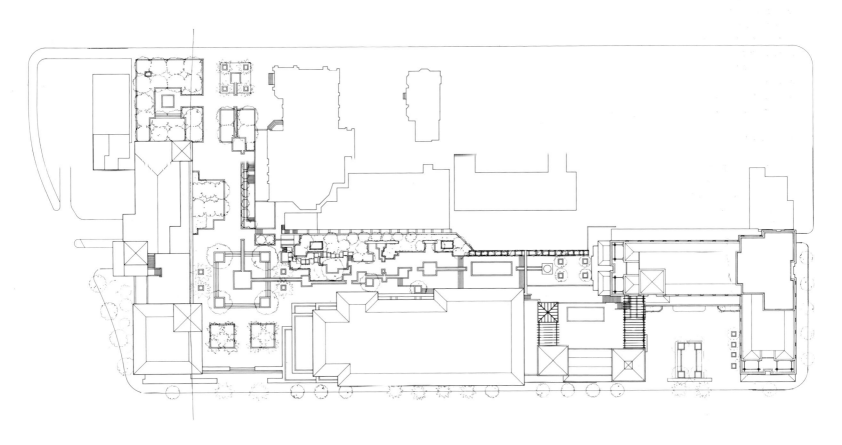

laboratory for design ideas, a literal and figurative bridge meant to reconcile oppositions in a programme requiring spaces for working as well as living, on a steeply sloping site in Santa Monica Canyon. To satisfy the difficult functional and physical requirements involved, the architects first created a sequence of stepping platforms that cascade down from a retaining wall stabilizing the street at the top of the hill, providing access to the main entrance. A rectilinear office and apartment block were then located on these terraces in order to take maximum advantage of ventilation and views, creating open spaces between them that are a reminder of Aline Barnsdall's dictum that the true Californian house should be just as much outside as inside. In the opaque patois favoured by many of their generation, the architects describe this exercise as being both 'about a house and a process, both of which explore the state of being in-between evolving ideas and formations. The state of being in-between is

fundamental to the program of the house, as it reflects the changing nature of living. The project offered the opportunity to explore the relationship between conception and representation through design and between perception and experience through construction as the work proceeded. The design developed and was enriched by discovery inherent in the experience of making the place. Transformation explores a technique for architectural design in the domain of both artifact and concept, parallelling the evolving nature of urban growth and change. The dialogue between the context of the past and a vision for the future frames the design process as a state of working in-between, in the elusive gap between history and possibility.'[11]

In a transformation of a totally different sort, Frank Dimster has undertaken the Herculean task of restoring the Villa Aurora, on the ethereal but treacherously unstable slopes of Pacific Palisades. Built by architect Mark Daniels in 1926, it was the

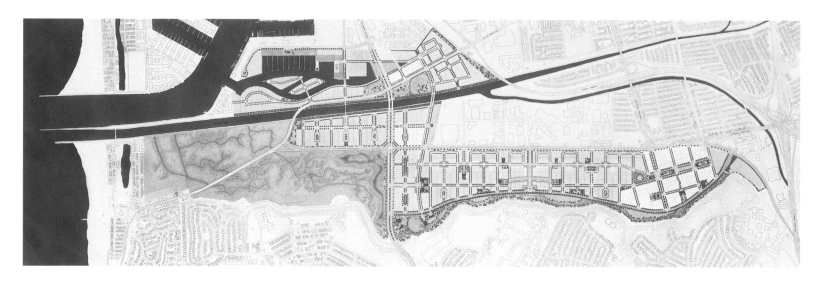

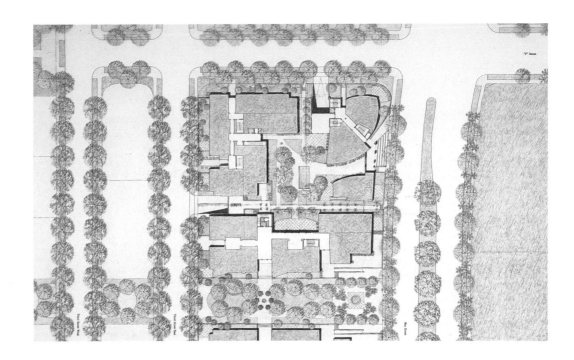

Playa Vista Development

Project, Los Angeles
Westside, 1989-93
Moore Ruble Yudell,
Hanna/Olin, Moule &
Polyzoides, Legorreta
Arquitectos, Andres Duaney
& Elizabeth Plater-Zyberk

Playa Vista is a proposed
mixed-use community that is
expected to be built on 957
acres adjacent to Westchester,
Playa del Rey, Venice, Marina
del Rey and Mar Vista. As
developers, Maguire Thomas
Partners assembled a multi-
disciplinary team consisting
of architects, landscape
architects, urban planners and
engineers, based on the ability
of each to suggest innovative
approaches. The site plan of
the neighbourhood structure
is by Moore Ruble Yudell.
The planning team became
involved in the Playa Vista
project early in 1989, and
met directly with each of the
community groups who had
opposed previous plans,
focusing on questions about
building heights, traffic and the
protection and expansion of
the Ballona Wetlands nature
preserve. A comprehensive
strategy was devised for
dealing with the delicate
ecological balance in the area,
which involves alternative
transportation systems and
a new mix of land uses, with
building groups organized in
low-rise configurations. The
residential studies illustrated
are by Moule & Polyzoides.

Harwood Lyon Dormitory
Pomona College, 1990
Moule & Polyzoides /
Peter deBretteville

As a dormitory addition
containing 80 new student
rooms, the building is
positioned along the northern
edge of an incomplete
quadrangle creating an
enclosed courtyard, as well
as two new courtyards on
the east and west. After
investigating the best historical
precedents, the architects
have provided a more
functional and lasting
alternative to the flimsy,
crowded student housing
that predominates in American
college architecture. By
incorporating open social
space into the ubiquitous linear
corridor, and using substantial,
durable, materials, they have
managed to elevate a
mundane building type into a
model against which future
additions to this campus, and
others, may be measured.

home of German writer Lion Feuchtwanger from
1944 until his death, when it was deeded to USC.
The rambling Mission Style house and library that
has accumulated there has now been purchased from
the University of Southern California by the German
government, which is converting it into an institute
sponsoring research, with accommodation for
scholars in residence. With meticulous attention to
detail, Dimster has brought the Villa Aurora, which
had been vacant and neglected for some time, back
to its original condition, while skilfully adding all of
the elements necessary to convert it to its new use.
The result is a preservationist's tour-de-force which
now stands as an accurate representation of an
important stylistic period in local history.

In nearby Santa Monica, Panos Koulermos goes
further back into the Mediterranean past, with a
proposal for a theatre in Santa Monica that has a
decidedly classical lineage. Arranging the seating of
the open-air auditorium in such a way that the framed
view through the stage is the Pacific itself, Koulermos
has replicated the original Greek intention of linking
near and distant views and landscape in a
straightforward and powerful way. In true Angelino

fashion, however, the base for the seating is a parking
garage rather than a gently sloping hillside dotted
with olive trees: one more reminder that the car is still
predominant in this city.

A multiple-use, residential office complex at 8291
Sunset Boulevard, by Charles Lagreco, has also been
designed to respond to vehicular movement along one
of the most famous thoroughfares in the world, as
well as to the juncture where the Los Angeles Basin
floor meets the city grid (a condition that has also
attracted the interest of Frank Israel). Spanning
between the two separate jurisdictions of the City
of Los Angeles and North Hollywood, the complex
had to address new planning guidelines that required
maximum provision for views, and encouraged
residential use in this area. Consequently, it organizes
both office and residential accommodation so that
each might have a southern exposure. Double-height
spaces first face the street at the lowest level and then
flip to the north , with the uppermost units designed
to take full advantage of an open roofscape. This
project is one more example of the creative solutions
now being put forward to explore the possibilities of
high density and mixed use throughout the city.

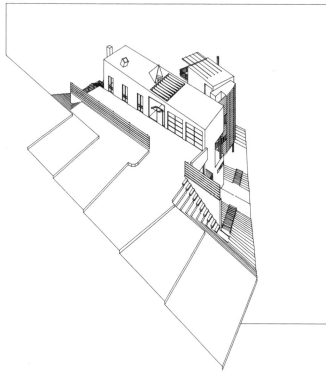

Villa Aurora
Pacific Palisades,
Restoration, 1993
Frank Dimster

Canyon House
Santa Monica Canyon, 1993
Cigolle Coleman
As both residence and office
for architects Mark Cigolle
and Katherine Coleman, this
house, located on a steeply
sloping site, is organized to
accommodate both
professional and domestic
activities. Important local
precursors of such an
arrangement, most notably
the Eames House and Studio,
have demonstrated that mixed-
use programmes of this type
can work quite successfully.
The result is a dramatic
juxtaposition of a lower, office
entrance element aligned with
the street and a second tall
tower, swinging away from it
to the west, accentuating the
two basic components in the
daily lives of a busy
contemporary couple.

The question of densities has also been explored
by John Mutlow in several projects, most notably in
Manhattan Place and Cabrillo Village. The first of
these represents a reinvestigation of the Los Angeles
courtyard prototype, intended to fit into an existing
inner-city urban fabric of older, large-scale apartment
buildings. The L-shaped project has a four-storey
south façade that aligns with a brick building to the
west, and an east elevation that conforms to a stucco
structure to the north. Community spaces at ground
level, at the corner, form the two residential wings,
anchoring the building to the street and providing
a social nucleus. Each cluster of six units forms a
single design element through the projection of
balconies, which also allows for economies in
concrete slab configuration.

Cabrillo Village, on the other hand, is on a
rural site in Saticoy, surrounded by lemon groves.
Originally a farm workers' camp, a series of
deteriorated board and batten cabins, built in the
1930s, were set to be demolished by the growers in
1975, until the farm workers acquired the camp,
rehabilitated the existing cabins, and expanded the
village to include a nursery school, a co-operative
food market, a chapel and new housing. The design
solution for these new units, as implemented by
Mutlow, is organized around a central green, which
steps down a slope and acts as a social space. All the
unit entrances face onto this green, and have a view
to the Sierre Madre Mountains to the north.
Aesthetically, the flat roofs and solid walls make
reference to Mexican adobe houses. Their massing,
sunshades and earth-related colours suggest
traditional architecture, and make the most of the
movement of the sun across the façade.

Stefanos Polyzoides, along with his partner
Elizabeth Moule (who does not teach at USC) have
been mentioned earlier in connection with their
involvement in the Playa Vista project and have
spent a great deal of time and effort in analyzing the
historic housing typologies of Los Angeles. Their
Arnaz Apartments project in Beverly Hills, which they
see as having provided the basis for many of the ideas
that they have put forward in the Maguire Thomas
development, has been used by them to examine the

concept of 'house', and how this can be incorporated in larger buildings. The Arnaz group is made up of 18 units, divided into three groups of six each, and resists the usual tendency of assembling individual units together, representing instead what James Stirling used to call a 'battery' building, which is very dense, with a unity that belies the specialized elements inside it. Because of the project's commercial basis, the architects began by taking the maximum envelope given to them by their developer client, and carving it out to form outside spaces; this is in keeping with their view of Los Angeles as a 'garden city' in which the outdoor component of a dwelling is just as important as its interior. As a result they have achieved the equivalent of 40 to 50 dwellings per acre here, showing that density need not necessarily be equated with a diminished lifestyle.

Their Marinos House, on the other hand, in Pacific Palisades, off Sunset Boulevard, is an investigation of 'houseness' at the most personal, detached level,

particularly as this relates to the topographic and environmental factors that are singularly identified with this area. Using as a guide the Kings Road House by Rudolph Schindler, in which several semi-unitary pieces are joined to focus attention on isolated parts of its site, Moule & Polyzoides have arranged disparate elements along a finger-like ridge, so that each will have a view forward to the Pacific, and seem to dissolve into, rather than present a challenge to, the landscape. The front piece of the building, nearest the street, is scaled to fit in with the surrounding neighbourhood, with functions of guest house and garage related to its location, whilst those pieces further along the ridge unfold to the back and side, and are rooted to the land, with framed views to the sea. The house was visualized by the architects as a Greek temple, in which there is an equilibrium established between architecture and landscape, as well as inside and outside, with the emphasis on the exterior reiterated once again.

Santa Monica Theatre
Project, Santa Monica, 1993
Panos Koulermos
In his proposal for a theatre in Santa Monica, Panos Koulermos strikes at the core of the question of a Mediterranean legacy in Los Angeles, and demonstrates where the term really began, with unmistakable associations with Classical Greek theatre forming the basis of the design. The connection with the distant landscape, which Vincent Scully in particular has shown to be an important part of that tradition, is essential here, also, with the Pacific framed as part of the stage backdrop, combining nature and architecture in a way that is reminiscent of the most historically significant contributors in the past.

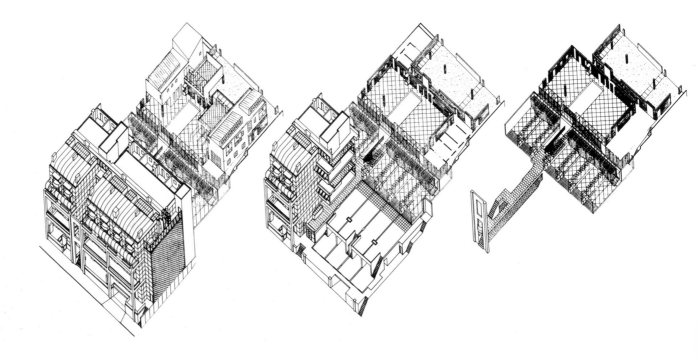

8291 Sunset Boulevard
North Hollywood, 1992
Charles Lagreco

Located directly opposite the site of Morphosis' Yuzen Car Museum, this mixed-use complex has quickly become a landmark on Sunset Boulevard, standing out from its eclectic surroundings because of its inherent order and quiet authority. The impression of permanence that it gives belies the difficulty that architect and client had in getting local authorities to accept the idea of combining commercial and residential uses in the same building – although this is now the hottest topic among architects and developers, who have suddenly realized that people actually prefer living near where they work, rather than spending 45 minutes on the freeway.

As an example of more public concerns, the Harwood Lyon Dormitory, by Moule & Polyzoides / Peter deBretteville, is an expression of social clustering of a different sort. Designed in the Jeffersonian tradition in which a campus is seen as an idealized city, the dormitory is positioned to complete an enclosed court, providing a wall on the southern edge of the campus that suggests an entrance, which did not exist previously, thus assuming a figurative identity for the entire institution. Using research gained from examining the most successful college dormitories in several countries, the architects have avoided the relentless corridors and isolated, warren-like rooms that seem to be the rule, and have clustered rooms around social spaces that are enlargements of wide circulation spaces. At the second floor level, rooms are also grouped around porches overlooking the green central court below. For durability, the building is built of concrete, which is sand-blasted to look like stone, and the red, green and grey palette of colours they have chosen echoes those used throughout the rest of the campus. It is a linear, normative structure, in which the ends are different, and used to tell the story of its function.

As the wide variety of this work illustrates, it is difficult to categorize the University of Southern California as following any specific theoretical direction. It is instead more constructive to note its reputation for providing a strong grounding in design fundamentals, offered by instructors such as Roger Sherwood, Graeme Morland, Frank Dimster, Panos Koulermos, John Mutlow, Marc Angelil and Ralph Knowles. And like Sci-Arc and UCLA it can boast of generations of architects who now make up a distinguished alumni, with many now practising in Los Angeles. Given the dramatic demographic and social changes now taking place in the city, each of these institutions, regardless of educational philosophy or pedagogical stance, is finding that they must take a position on the direction of its future growth. Many of those involved have already done so, realizing that the staggering problems that now exist also present great opportunities for change. It is over the question of the nature of that change that sides are now being drawn.

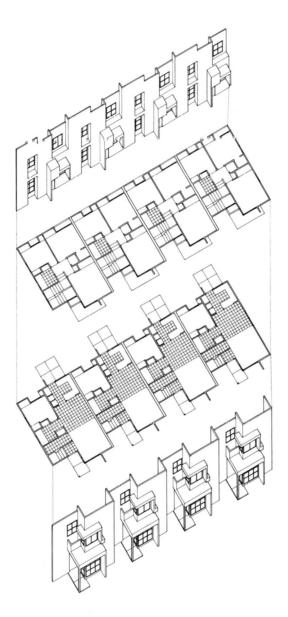

Cabrillo Village
Saticoy, 1990
John Mutlow
Cabrillo Village occupies a rural site surrounded by lemon groves. Mutlow's housing forms an extension to a farm workers' camp, built originally in the 1930s, and acquired from the owners by a farm workers' cooperative in the mid-1970s. The new houses are organized around a central green which gives the village a social focus and enjoys views of the mountains to the north. There are six different unit types with two, three and four bedroom configurations; the repetitive nature of the stepped plan allows for a more varied design than would a formal rectangular arrangement. The two-storey row houses have front yards and rear gardens with two-car car ports attached.

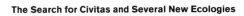

The Search for Civitas and Several New Ecologies

Important as the ideological warfare now going on between various architectural factions may seem to those involved in its seemingly endless skirmishes, or to the media, who thrive on reporting the latest weaponry used, it is necessary to keep them in perspective, by concluding with an overview of some significant changes that have taken place in Los Angeles. These are destined to alter completely the public image, held throughout the world, of the city as halcyon nirvana by the edge of the Pacific, and the source of every new and trendy trend. To begin to gain that perspective, it should first be noted that there is a discernible tendency at the moment to predict the eclipse of American power, which many believe has already taken place, as the century of the 'era of Asia' begins. Los Angeles, as the focal microcosm of America's national aspirations and its collective psyche, has been cited as the paragon of this decline. As Ivan Fallon puts it: 'Los Angeles typifies and magnifies every American dilemma, as well as every American dream.'[1] It is a city which has become the Ellis Island of the nineties as 600,000 immigrants, legal and illegal, flood in from Mexico and South America every year. It is a city of black and mixed-

Downtown Los Angeles
Now that Los Angeles has
assumed the title of 'capital' of
the West Coast, a suitably
vertical profile of skyscrapers,
is considered to be of the
utmost importance for the
downtown area. Downtown
Los Angeles is where the
city began in 1789 and it
is becoming increasingly
prominent as a cultural and
financial focus. Not only is
it composed of powerful
corporate interests, but it
forms an industrial base that
employs more than 60,000
people and generates upwards
of $12 billion annually. It is
also home to diverse
residential interests. Ringing
the downtown are various
long-established, ethnically-
based communities such as
South Central, Chinatown
and Little Tokyo.

race ghettos at one end of town and, at the other,
prosperous walled-off enclaves where the 'haves' live
behind security guards. It is also a city of 'soaring
unemployment ... of paralyzing bureaucracy and over-
regulation and even more fundamental problems.'[2]
Those 'fundamental problems' all revolve around the
virtual disenfranchisement of a vast segment of inner-
city poor in South Central and East Los Angeles, in
a zone that has been red-lined by banks, creating
a vicious cycle of degradation, and periodic civil
violence. Naysayers, who are pessimistic about the
possibility of a bright future for the city, respond
to a disparity that is apparent everywhere: of
a conurbation that is dynamic and socially
heterogeneous on the one hand, but beset by crippling
problems on the other. Revelations that seem to
surface with disturbing rapidity – of a system of
organized communities of thousands of homeless
discovered living under a freeway one day, followed
by an exposé on the netherworld of crack dealers and
prostitutes who service the semi-drivers using
transport centres in Little Tokyo the next – play
against the now-familiar refrain of the latest atrocities
carried out by street gangs such as the Crips and
Bloods, and seem to lend credence to such views,
making Belfast seem calm by comparison.

The homeless in Los Angeles – who seem to be
metastasizing daily in spite of numerous, well-
intentioned but disorganized attempts to help them –
are dispersed around the city, with particularly
noticeable concentrations along freeway on-ramps,
where drivers must stop for metered lights that
stagger entry. They remain a graphic reminder of the
marginally thin line between inclusion and exclusion
in a pitiless society now having to run faster to stay in
what only seems to be the same place. The homeless
lining the ramps in the East Central area are simply
'down on their luck for one reason or other'
according to a government-appointed commission
which, having been assembled to outline what Los
Angeles might be like the year 2000, has glossed over
their plight in an extremely patronizing official
document.[3] The attitude taken in their report, *Los
Angeles 2000: A City for the Future*, is characteristic
of the disdain and indifference of a society weakened,

in the words of veteran news presenter John
Chancellor, 'by a thousand wounds we find difficult to
heal. We have weakened ourselves in the way we
practise our politics, manage our businesses, teach our
children, succour our poor, care for our elders, save
our money, protect our environment and run our
government.'[4] Living rough, out on the street, is the
final step in an almost imperceptible process of social
disenfranchisement in which, as Jean Baudrillard has
said: 'You lose your rights one by one; first your job,
then your car. And when your driver's licence goes,
so does your identity.'[5]

The symptoms of this withdrawal may be
identified in some of the unwittingly ironic and
pathetically inadequate gestures of help that are made
to the homeless, such as one recent official offer of
individual shopping carts, personalized with engraved
name plates to discourage theft of the rolling transport
favoured by street people, to keep them and their few
possessions on the move, so as to avoid being arrested
for vagrancy. Another is an annual pricey tour of
architectural masterpieces in stylish Brentwood and
Bel-Air, with proceeds going to the homeless, in which
the irony of tours of the homes of the rich to help the
homeless is totally missed. The final irony presented
by the phalanx of homeless lining the freeway ramps,
is that this is the most critical confrontation that can
take place between society's participants and its
outcasts, since the car is an extension of the home for
a majority of Angelenos and its repossession is one of
the last stages before marginality.

The finality of such disenfranchisement is a
graphic reminder that, for the moment, the freeway
still remains the one common, public space in the city,
confirming some sociologists' belief that in America,
unlike Europe, the public realm really consists of a
recurring event, rather than a grouping of buildings.
In Los Angeles, that recurring event is rush hour. As
Jean Baudrillard has indicated, traffic reaches a level
of dramatic attraction on Los Angeles freeways not
seen anywhere else in the world, to the extent that it
has attained the status of symbolic organization, as a
'collective game'.[6] In this 'collective propulsion',
social membership is validated by reading signs
overhead, and dots an dashes on the road, 'which

gives you an extraordinary feeling of instant lucidity...of a functional participation that is reflected in certain precise gestures, pure statistical energy, a ritual being acted out.' It is the same ritual, in fact, as that which has previously been shown to now be devoid of all traditional meaning, as a means of collective survival.[7]

The subliminal power of that sense, along with the reluctance of people to give up the machine that makes it possible to participate in it, explains why most attempts to design public space, in the European tradition, have failed here in the past. As researchers who are now finding success in teaching languages will testify, since raised adrenaline levels imprint knowledge more indelibly than any other method, the excitement caused by weaving in and out of five lanes of cars moving at more than 80 miles an hour is addictive to many, for whom a bus is a pallid substitute. In this public space, each car is a building or, more accurately, a self-contained mobile house with its occupants oblivious to the world outside. If there is an external image that does register, it is that there is finally an appropriate, Emerald City outline of the downtown skyline in the distance, or of Glendale, Pasadena, Burbank or Santa Monica, now suitably suggestive of the profile of what a city should look like.[8] The obsolescence of the freeway has increased the probability of traffic jams, increasing sales of cellular phones, books on tape, and even dashboard-mounted miniature televisions, intended to while away the hours. While the freeways are abstracted into a series of numbers such as 5, 10, 110 and 405, the vanity plate, as a characteristically Californian phenomenon, allows personalization of the car. These plates, which cost more than those normally issued, reveal much about the need to communicate, and the willingness to pay to do so within the limits of the seven characters allowed. The range of imagination is impressive, as for example in the attempt to outwit the department of motor vehicle censors by correctly assuming that they don't speak French, as well as a pre-emptive strike at tailgaters who do (MERDTET), or in the creative use of numbers to advertise personal characteristics (I CRE 8, GR8LEGS, HOTDA8), and the nostalgic plate on a '56 Corvette (I WAS I 2).

First Interstate World Center
Downtown Los Angeles, 1990
Pei Cobb Freed & Partners
The 73-storey First Interstate World Center tower, is the tallest on the West Coast. It has been shaped to create a memorable image on the skyline and yet grant primacy at street level to Bertram Goodhue's great library. Related goals include the reinforcement of the surrounding area as the heart of downtown, and remaking the vital pedestrian connection between the two previously separated parts of Los Angeles made possible by the creation of the Bunker Hill Steps. The First Interstate World Center makes its presence felt at street level not as a self-centered object but rather as one of several supporting actors in an urban scene whose unquestioned star is the historic library.

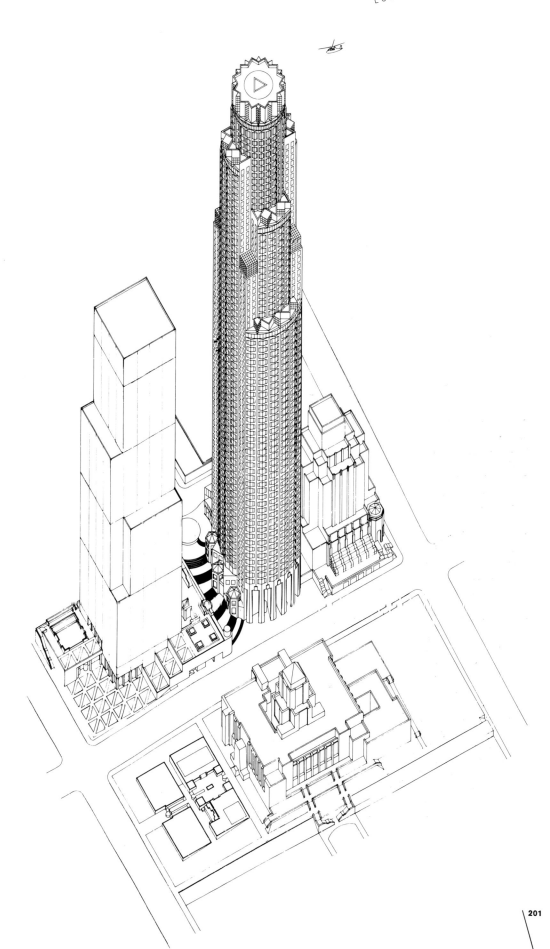

Crocker Center
Downtown Los Angeles,
1993
Skidmore, Owings & Merrill

First Interstate World Center
The plan form of the First Interstate World Center tower is derived from a matrix of two overlapping and concentric geometries to produce, in effect, a squared circle. The matrix helps to organize the site and shape the building to respond to its specific requirements. The square makes for optimum useable floor plates and the circle, for an urbane and neighbourly stance. The combination creates a visual richness and an architectural character intended to distinguish the tower as a special place both from nearby on the city streets and from afar at high speed on the freeway.

Periodic eruptions of civic violence in Los Angeles underscore extensive reliance on the freeways there, and their social importance was drawn clearly in an interview with talk show host Arsenio Hall, conducted by Rod Lurie. Lurie began by describing the scene during the Spring '92 'uprising' as 'Riot Night: smoke, death, Reginald Denny, heroism, the apocalypse and Arsenio – quite literally the only show in town. With the exception of the E! Channel, which was interviewing people in the street about their celebrity double, every station in Los Angeles was presenting what we can only call "the images". The city had shut down.' He then asked Hall how he had managed to get Mayor Bradley on the show, and he answered: 'I called and called and called. I was not going to take no for an answer. He was very busy, but as soon as I got him on the phone, the first and only thing that came out of his mouth was "yes"... I put together a simulcast on several radio stations. My thing was, I gotta get to people in cars.'[9]

The changes that have taken place in Autopia, which is the least contextual of Banham's 'Four Ecologies', begin to suggest further addenda which would make the contemporary picture more complete, and several have already been put forward by other observers of the city.

Peter Plagens, in his vitriolic *Ecology of Evil*, begins to hint at the overwhelming social changes that have occurred there in the last 25 years, and in a reference to the tendency of visitors always to see Los Angeles as a paradise, makes counterpoints that take on additional relevance today.[10] Plagens begins his refutation by attacking the notion that the freeway system is an inevitable fact of life, one which should not only be tolerated but appreciated as a contemporary art form. Citing the pervasiveness of the self-fulfilling myth that such a system perpetuates by assuming that 'everyone has a car or that it is a civic duty to own one', Plagens gets to the heart of the matter: 'The assumption that near-universal automobile ownership is near-universal happiness,' he says, 'couldn't be more in error. You have a car in LA not because you want one...but because there simply isn't any choice. You must buy all that metal, rubber and gas for your very own; endlessly pilot your own

ship and ride your own shotgun and eternally keep that weathered throttle to the floor to keep the bastard behind you off your bumper. It is absolute madness.'[11] The evil in this – aside from the insidiousness of the Highway Trust Fund, which is separate from California's general revenue fund, fed by a gas tax and used to build more freeways and generate the need for more gas in an endless spiral – is the smog which remains unchecked by a flawed smog check system, and the tragedy of some of the most beautiful landscape in America being covered in a carpet of asphalt.[12] In all his outrage, however, Plagens only hints at the deeper evil inherent in this environment, which he finally determines is 'an elusive place: all flesh and no soul, all buildings and no architecture, all property and no land, all billboards and nothing to say, all ideas and no principles, containing only brief, veiled references to the degree of distortion of the mind and spirit that is endemic here.'[13] Few have ever got to grips with this pervasive sense of rot which Los Angeles, for all of its endless, superficial self-promotion, seems to incubate, and the 'Ecology of Evil' goes much further than the freeway.

Mike Davis, with his penchant for what Richard Weinstein has characterized as 'turning rocks over to see the insects underneath', is its most relentless chronicler, as are David Lynch in *Blue Velvet*, and Kim Stanley Robinson in *The Gold Coast*. But for sheer, microscopic veracity, few can top Joan Didion in books such as *Play it as it Lays*, *Run River*, and *Slouching Toward Bethlehem*, each of which isolate a different aspect of the city.[14] Having grown up in Sacramento, studied at Berkeley and come back to Los Angeles in the late 1960s after a brief stay in New York City, Didion shares the insights of a native Californian, but goes beyond the clearly drawn contrasts of life in this city as an institutionalized war game played out between various classes and factions, into the more complex realm of causality and motive. Maria Wyeth, the heroine of *Play it as it Lays,* for example, is used by Didion in a thinly concealed autobiographical way, as a literary device for examining the uncertainty of social institutions today. Her belief that life is aleatory and that evil lives in

Los Angeles Public Library
Downtown Los Angeles,
1926, Bertram Goodhue

Bunker Hill Steps
Downtown Los Angeles,
1983, Lawrence Halprin
This ambitious project
reconnects the upper and
lower portions of Bunker Hill,
which were made inaccessible
when a much loved funicular
was dismantled nearly 50
years ago. Seen in this
perspective drawing by Moule
& Polyzoides, Lawrence
Halprin's monumental
staircase is closely integrated
with the surrounding buildings.
Developed in close
collaboration with I.M. Pei,
who designed the adjacent
First Interstate World Center,
the steps feed into the new
skyscraper at various levels
which form small plazas, with
outdoor cafés, planted seating
areas and fountains.

hidden, unexpected places, leads to the conclusion that Los Angeles exemplifies the shattering of the myth of America's supernatural compact, subconsciously continued from its God-fearing, agrarian past.[15]

Didion continues to be invoked in extreme moments of civic soul-searching, such as those following the 'uprising' of 1992, when social critics such as Kevin Starr and Mike Davis began to sift through the past in search of clues to the problems of the present. In addition to noting that the *persona fictiva* of Los Angeles remains that of the feminine religious image that the Franciscans imprinted on it, and pointing out the contemporary relevance of the Catholic diametrics of salvation/redemption or heaven/hell to civic schizophrenia at the moment, Starr has frequently made the point that the 'multiple yet synchronic' urban character of the region, firmly established by film makers, and novelists such as Christopher Isherwood, Nathanael West and Raymond Chandler, makes its image bounce about like the fragments defined in high particle physics, which are characterized by disassociation and re-combination.[16]

Mike Davis has invoked Didion in another way, speaking of the continuous struggle for open space that has always gone on in the region, captured best by Didion in her description of dispossession in *The Notes of a Native Daughter*. One of Davis' most memorable images has been his recollection of 'the world we have lost since World War II, and the contradiction of the natural resources that were California's biggest asset.'[17] The most graphic changes, in his view, have been in the so-called Inland Empire, from San Diego to Santa Barbara, where orange groves were once so abundant that they converted a semi-desert landscape into a paradise. As Carey McWilliams has described them: 'The appearance of orange and lemon groves in such a land was as pleasing to the eye as the sight of an oasis in the desert. The evergreen and fragrant belts of citrus trees tended to compensate for the dryness; the heat, the scorched earth of the long summers.'[18] Orange County was the richest agricultural area in the United States but has now been systematically decimated by

development, which has changed its fragile micro-climate beyond recognition.[19] From this example, of the destruction of a region that had once come to symbolize the entire state, Davis has also focused on the question of parks in Los Angeles, which he has said has 'less open space than any city in America.'[20] Drawing comparisons with New York City, he has noted that the landscape architect Frederick Law Olmsted, after his triumph at Central Park, was commissioned to prepare a similar plan for Los Angeles, which was significant in its imaginative treatment of the flooding which typically occurs after winter storms, wasting precious rainwater that could ensure the continual maintenance of green space. The plan was unfortunately never implemented and the city was covered in concrete, exacerbating the flooding problem even further. The destruction of the Los Angeles River was part of this process. Due to the strength of industrial interests, the cost of restoring parts of it to its original condition, as a necessary first step in what is now seen as the need finally to provide the city with green space, is estimated at more than one billion dollars.

As an antidote to what Davis has described as 'the impoverished public realm', and to the 'Ecology of Evil' that Peter Plagens has identified as having emerged out of Banham's Autopia, Proposition C now indicates that the freeway gridlock is beginning to break up. This initiative, approved by referendum, involved a half-cent sales tax rise for use on public transportation. Since its inception in 1990, Proposition C has generated 30 billion dollars in revenue, allowing the Los Angeles County Transportation Commission to become responsible for the largest public works project in the United States. The commission now has the enviable task of having to spend one billion dollars a year on public transportation. The plan includes subways, light and heavy rail surface trains, buses, electric trolley buses, zones for reduced taxi fares, high-occupancy carpool lanes, and a transportation-demand management system to monitor ride-sharing and to control parking. An air quality plan, imposed by the Environmental Protection Agency, has required that bus emissions be cut by 30 per cent before the year

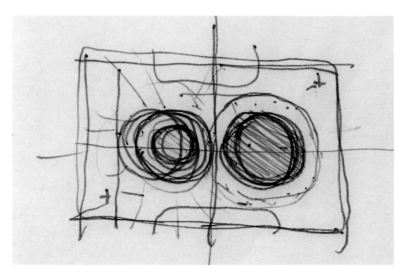
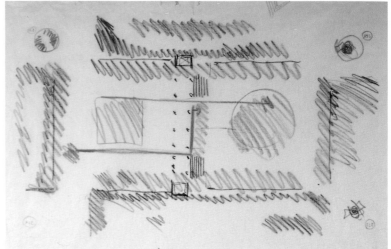

Pershing Square
Downtown Los Angeles,
1993
Ricardo Legorreta and
Hanna /Olin
Once the place to promenade
in downtown Los Angeles,
Pershing Square had
disintegrated into desolation by
1950, when its stately queen
palms were removed to Griffith
Park. After a failed attempt in
the mid-1980s to reclaim the
entire city block from the drug
pushers, addicts, prostitutes
and the homeless that had
taken it over, architect Ricardo
Legoretta and landscape
architects Hanna/Olin were
invited to submit proposals.
Their scheme invites
pedestrians back into the
space. A new fountain acts
as a sculptural landmark,
giving the park a new identity,
and the queen palms are
back in Pershing Square,
which has become an
important symbol of change
in the downtown area.

2000, and one hundred per cent by 2010.
Surprisingly, Los Angeles has the highest passenger
usage per mile of any transport system in the United
States, typically made up of the poor, who cannot
afford cars. The electrification of this entire, heavily
used system, will require power poles and lines along
18 routes, combined with a massive landscape
programme intended to camouflage the results.

In a Horatio Alger scenario combining skill, luck
and opportunity, architect Douglas Suisman, who has
written on the Los Angeles boulevard, contacted Nick
Patsaouras, on the board of the Southern California
Rapid Transit District, offering the services of his
firm, Public Works, to help with this effort. Within
three weeks, Suisman was presenting ideas for
'A New Streetscape for Los Angeles', involving an
integrated plan to minimize the visual effect of the
maze of wires required for electric trolleys, and the
high cost of installation and maintenance of
landscaping the estimated 30,000 trees that would be
required. Suisman speaks energetically about cities,
and particularly streets, which he describes as the
'lens' that focuses discussion of the political and
sociological life of any urban area. Having moved

to Los Angeles from New York, like Frank Israel, he
has also been struck by the difference in scale between
the two cities, as well as the lack of intermediate
texture between freeway, street and neighbourhood,
caused by rapid growth. In trying to come to grips
with this different perception of scale, which he
characterizes as 'the fundamental dilemma of Los
Angeles', Suisman eventually settled on the boulevard
as a means of unravelling it, and set out to discover
why this street type has developed as it has, without
becoming as vital as its European counterpart. His
subsequent study, which begins with the rhetorical
question: 'Can a city be a city without appearing to
be one?', ends up as a paean to a street form which,
he feels, is the only real alternative to the public space
of the freeway. This is because, as he notes: 'Public
space by definition must allow for the widest range
of activities and behaviour for the widest group of
people...and this definition surely lays to rest the
occasional claims that in Los Angeles, the public
realm is to be found on the freeways and beaches.'[21]

The political problems that have arisen from the
planned transit revolution say much about the current
mental map of the city and the various factions in it,

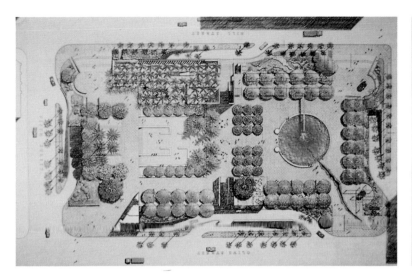

and the truth inherent in the contention that the neighbourhoods, rather than the suburbs, now govern. Rather than an ecology of enclaves, it is now one of neighbourhoods which may give a sense of identity in future. Questions about rights of way, and controversies over routing, in which every mile has been contested, have revealed the true territorial boundaries in Los Angeles today, and the difficulty involved in changing the current public perception of buses as a conveyance of the poor has shown that the mania for the car will be hard to alter. Visions of gangs riding subways from South Central into wealthy communities to the north and west, and the mental categorization of buses as second-class transportation, are difficult to change, but there is a high level of interest in establishing such a system and a great deal of determination being channelled into the effort to overcome the racial, social and economic agendas of the enclaves. To assist in this, Suisman has emphasized the importance of linking transportation to planning and land-use policy, and of making the entire system comprehensive enough to approximate the convenience of a car in covering such a large area. Attrition will eventually eliminate cars that cannot

meet increasingly stringent emission standards, and a buy-back policy similar to that already proven effective in other cities such as Athens (where government subsidies are given if old cars are turned in, to purchase new, less polluting vehicles), as well as encouraging progress on electric cars, points toward an entirely different kind of freeway in the future.

The suburban model, and the automobile that made it possible, have little chance of carrying on as they have done, both because of the changing sense that Los Angeles should be socially integrated and have a centre, and the realization at many levels that adaptation to a condensed urban prototype is not only advantageous, but necessary. This new ecology of the neighbourhood, which Banham hinted at as a possibility, but glossed over too quickly, looks set eventually to supersede his Surfurbia, with projects like Playa Vista pointing the way.

Following the new ecologies of Evil and Neighbourhood, the third ecology which has burgeoned recently is 'Downtown'; now deemed to be urgently necessary in a city frequently referred to as the capital of the West Coast, or even the Pacific Rim, a suitably vertical three-dimensional profile of

**Museum of
Contemporary Art**
Downtown Los Angeles,
1986, Arata Isozaki
Taken in the context of
previous museums designed
by this architect, MOCA
represents a critical juncture,
both as a synthesis of formal
preoccupations seen
elsewhere and a determined
effort to establish a new
language. Isozaki's reliance
on platonic solids is still very
much in evidence here, with
the semi-circular vaults that
first surfaced in the Fujimi
Clubhouse and the Kitakyushu
Central Library in the early
1970s dominating the roof.
The omnipresent cube, which
can be traced in every one of
his buildings from the Oita
Prefectural Library of 1966
onwards, is also a major part
of his formal vocabulary, as is
the pyramid, which is used to
light the galleries.

skyscrapers, as well as appropriate centres of cultural activities, is considered to be of utmost importance. As described by Robert Harris, former dean of the School of Architecture at the University of Southern California: 'Downtown Los Angeles – where the city began in 1789 – is indeed a prominent centre. Not only is Downtown composed of powerful corporate interests, but it is also an industrial base that directly employs more than 60,000 people and generates upwards of $12 billion annually. Additionally, it is home to diverse residential communities, ranging from a historic community in the heart of the industrial district to apartment and condominium concentrations in Bunker Hill and South Park. Ringing the downtown are various long-established, ethnically-based residential communities such as Chinatown, Little Tokyo, East Los Angeles, Echo Park, South Central, and Pico Union.'[22]

Far and away the most visible, and identifiable, addition to the Los Angeles downtown is the First Interstate World Center by Pei Cobb Freed & Partners, for Maguire Thomas as client, commonly known locally as the 'Library Tower', completed in 1990. This singular, hub-like equivalent of New York's World Trade Center is located across the street from the Los Angeles Public Library of 1926 by Bertram Goodhue, which was threatened with demolition until an agreement was reached by which the client could purchase air rights from the city. This allowed the library to be preserved and the tower to reach its desired commanding height. The 73-storey tower is consequently the highest on the West Coast and, as the architect has described it, 'is based on a matrix of overlapping and concentric geometries, one circular and the other orthogonal, which define the building through a series of setbacks as it climbs to its full 1018-foot height. The tower has been shaped to create a memorable image on the skyline and yet grant primacy at street level to Goodhue's great library. Related goals include reinforcement of the area surrounding the library as the heart of downtown, and the vital connection between two previously separated parts of Los Angeles. The creation of the Bunker Hill Steps affords the only direct pedestrian access between the upper and lower

parts of downtown.'[23] Bordered by 5th Street on the south, which is where the library is located, and Hope Street on the north, with a 50-foot change in elevation up to Bunker Hill taking place within its boundaries, the tower site offered a complex set of design circumstances, not least of which was to recreate a link once provided by a fondly remembered funicular which traversed the hill near this point. Landscape architect Lawrence Halprin of San Francisco provided a variant of the Spanish Steps in Rome to solve what had been an intractable problem, with technological help from exterior escalators along a massive retaining wall supporting the 50-foot incline. Three separate landings, treated as individual plazas, are joined by a central waterfall with cafés and shops grouped into outdoor pavilions at each level. These lead directly into public retail areas inside the tower, and to the elevators, in an imaginative attempt to break away from the hermetic isolation that has frequently plagued high rises in the past.

Divided into five typical floor plans, the tower begins with a rectilinear plan, with rounded corners intended to be more complementary to the library nearby. Only the top, circular floor is a platonic solid, its purity augmented by faceted stone and glass that is particularly effective at sunset. Designed to withstand an earthquake of magnitude 8.3 on the Richter scale, since it is only 33 miles from the San Andreas fault, the tower uses an innovative dual frame engineered to deal with the contradictory demands of earth tremors, which call for structural flexibility, and wind load, which requires stiffness for resistance. The system includes a steel frame on the exterior perimeter, designed for ductility against seismic shock, and a rigid 74-foot-square steel core which runs the full height of the building. The curtain wall effectiveness of this structure is most clearly felt at street level which, as the architect explains, 'because of its necessarily small footprint and the number of elevators required to serve a building of such great height ... has only a limited amount of space for public use. To make the transition from street to lobby seem less constrained, a series of sequential spaces have been established. Arrival and departure are orchestrated as experiential events.'[24]

As two of the major centrepieces of the new downtown image, it is interesting that Gehry's Disney Concert Hall and the Library Tower were both designed to permit direct access from the street, and this concern had much to do with their final form. Considering Los Angeles' past reputation as a car-orientated, insular city that is impossible for pedestrians to negotiate, the significance of such attention becomes apparent, as evidence of a determined effort to change this image and to create new urban symbols that work at street level.

In a happy civic coincidence, plans to rehabilitate Pershing Square, situated near the Library Tower, have now been finalized. This project will guarantee the completion of another piece of the downtown puzzle, and bring this entire area one step closer to the image that urban redevelopers now believe it should have. At the turn of the century the square, which is bounded by 5th, 6th, Olive and Hill Streets, was a lush, verdant oasis of elongated queen palms, interspersed with pedestrian pathways that criss-crossed it from corner to corner. Fifty years on, the palms had been removed, and the 'park' was simply a cover for the garage beneath it, cut off from the city by access ramps to the parking level below. Families out for a Sunday stroll had been replaced by drug pushers and prostitutes, and there were frequent confrontations between the police and the homeless who erected cardboard shelters there.

After a competition sponsored by the Pershing Square Management Association fell through in 1985, the Pershing Square Neighborhood Association became involved, and commissioned the Mexican architect Ricardo Legorreta to re-examine the area, along with landscape architects Hanna/Olin. Together, they began to identify elements basic to the success of any urban park in their experience, regardless of location, and arrived at four elemental ingredients. People, as the first of these, are also the most elusive, since they are the most difficult to predict, especially in a city that is not known for public spaces. However, it is hoped that the opening up of Halprin's stairway as a link to Bunker Hill, and the relative proximity of a traditional Hispanic market, will encourage visitors to the park, and the basic design approach, of removing the vehicular barriers that had existed around the park's edge, has been conceived with this in mind. As refinements to the strategy of openness of the perimeter to people rather than cars, Hanna/Olin and Legoretta activated each corner of the rectangular site, and identified a natural line of demarcation or movement across its centre which could be used to divide it into segments, in order to reduce its scale. A ten-foot slope from one end of the square to the other also indicates the possibility of an upper and lower part of the park, with the space between them being a point of access to the parking level which has remained. Legoretta's love of colour emerges here in a dramatic statement as a 125-foot-high purple tower which marks this point of transition, intended as a landmark for the entire downtown area. An aqueduct which is connected to it supplies water for a circular fountain around its base.

By opening up the corners of the rectangle, which is made possible by a stricter configuration of the ramps leading down to the underground parking garage, Pershing Square has been returned to the city once again. Raised *allées* of trees, with integral seating running their entire length, are intended to invite people to spend time here, and the transit station nearby will also make people more aware of the park. The queen palms that had been on the site and were later removed to Griffith Park, have now been returned, as a symbol that Pershing Square has itself been returned to the people.

In addition to its lack of public parks, the downtown area of Los Angeles has also been conspicuously deprived of cultural institutions in the recent past. The Dorothy Chandler Pavilion, which has been the home of the Los Angeles Philharmonic, has now become too small effectively to serve this role. An important signal of the coincidental effort to establish downtown as a strong cultural centre is the construction of Gehry's Walt Disney Concert Hall, scheduled for completion in 1996. Controversy has characterized the work of Frank Gehry from the start – indeed he has willingly sought it out in order to get across his social message – so the ripple that resulted from his release of the Disney Concert Hall design should have come as no surprise. What was

Museum of Contemporary Art

The museum today looks diminutive in comparison to the office towers, hotels and housing blocks around it. The great majority of MOCA's accommodation is set into the vast parking levels of California Plaza, so that only the vaulted library (which acts as a gateway to the museum) and the pyramids that identify the galleries are visible from Grand Avenue.

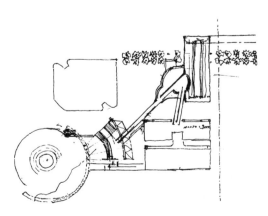

surprising, however, and quite unexpected, was that the majority of the criticism should have come from the public rather than the architectural profession: it has been levelled by the 'average Angelenos' whose complex psyches this architect is supposed to understand best. Instead of the 'undulating walls' which ' seem to be blown along in a breeze', or the 'majestic galleon in full sail' that was so consistently praised in the *Los Angeles Sunday Times* after the initial model was presented, the person on the street has interpreted the Concert Hall as a gigantic piece of caramel seeming to melt in the noonday sun.[25] Metaphorical misreadings of this sort have been relegated by most historians to late Modernism, when buildings such as Jørn Utzon's Sydney Opera House, intended to represent white sails in the sunset, became 'a scrum of nuns' to everyday Australians. Therein lies a clue to this debate.

Having begun in typical Gehry fashion, with four disjointed volumes rendered in completely different materials connected only by the functional logic of their individual massing, the Disney Concert Hall has slowly come to conform to the twin constraints imposed by acoustics and property lines. In response to an original competition directive to design the Concert Hall in the shape of a drum, Gehry's first scheme proposed three spiralling limestone-clad balconies. These led the eye gradually upwards from a diminutive entrance covered by a ball-like form, elegantly rendered in faceted glass panels, towards a fly-tower above the stage. The solidity of this stone spiral was offset by a 'conservatory' of angular glass that swept up from the base line running alongside the entrance pavilion, to a high-point braced by a stylized acropolis, approximating the roof lines of the Dorothy Chandler Pavilion across the street. Each piece of Gehry's winning competition entry seemed to complement the other, by playing off hard against soft, fragile against durable and monumental against ephemeral. Following the award of the commission, a new acoustic consultant took over, who required that the circular form of the hall be changed to a rectangle, with walls tilting inward and a concave ceiling installed to improve the sound. This radical shift, along with the spectacular addition of the Ritz

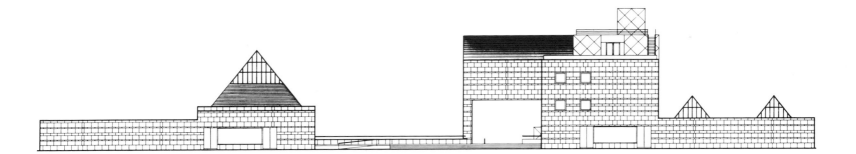

**Museum of
Contemporary Art**

Since its completion, MOCA
has been consistently selected
as one of the top ten favourite
buildings by American
architects. It has also provided
a focal point of civic pride for a
city that is slowly beginning to
try to live up to its designation
of 'cultural capital of the West
Coast', and is tangible proof
that Isozaki's history lessons
have had a lasting civic effect.

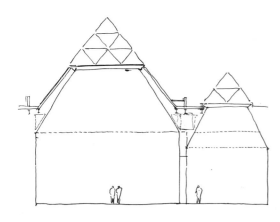

Carlton Hotel to the site (since withdrawn), forced a
new strategy. The result is a more uniformly
monolithic building, with the fragility and angularity
of the lost and lamented conservatory replaced by a
serpentine streetside arcade and the crocus-shaped
towers that hide the acoustician's shoebox inside.

In a presentation at Sci-Arc in December of 1991,
shortly after the unified scheme for the Disney Hall
was unveiled, Elizabeth Plater-Zyberk noted that the
'single building syndrome' is alive and well in Los
Angeles, and that the majority of architects continue
to focus on an isolated monument to the detriment of
urban interaction, community and context. For Frank
Gehry, however, whose tectonics represents an
attempt to break down this monumental approach in
order more accurately to reflect the low-scaled eclectic
cityscape of Los Angeles, the Disney Concert Hall
represents a singularity made necessary by
circumstance and is obviously an anomaly to those
who have mistakenly labelled his urban readings as
'Deconstructive' in the past. The public misreadings
of the form of the Concert Hall are the inevitable
result of having made such a dramatic step into
previously uncharted formal territory, and are also a

sign of Gehry's functionalism, since they can be
equated with the mis-read metaphors of Modernism.

Gehry's recent string of public buildings provides
a seductive, stylistic alternative to other directions in
the city today. While not neo-Modern, in the sense
that they try to improve on the Modernist aesthetic as
formal expressions of function, they are sculptured
'objects' to be appreciated as three-dimensional works
of art. As they continue to move away from any
possible confusion with Deconstructivism, they
especially appeal to those disillusioned with the
defensive posture much new architecture has taken,
and the profusion of theories being bandied about
today. They celebrate form, and the making of it,
for its own sake, and as Gehry continues to feel less
self-conscious about his acceptance of fine materials,
the sophistication of those forms is a constant source
of delight. Bunker Hill will soon have its long awaited
cultural symbol and if the architect has his way, that
symbol will be more accessible than any Concert
Hall has ever been in the past. The memory of Walt
Disney will thus be honoured with an architectural
'Fantasia' beyond the imagination of anyone but
Frank Gehry and Disney himself.

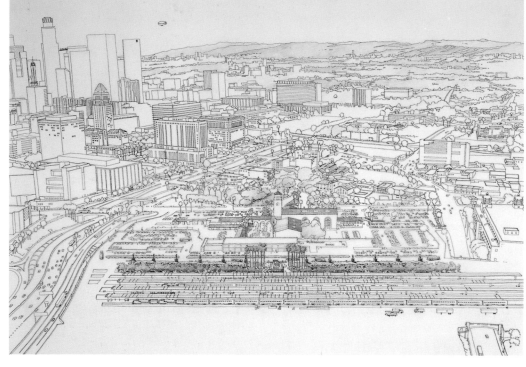

Union Station
Downtown Los Angeles,
1934-39
John and Donald Parkinson

Downtown Strategic Plan
Moule & Polyzoides
In speaking about the state of
the 'downtown' in cities across
America today, Elizabeth
Moule, who as partner with
Stefanos Polyzoides has been
involved in the formulation of
the new Downtown Strategic
Plan for Los Angeles as part of
a consortium of other architects
and planners, passionately
invokes the 'common meeting
ground' which she feels has
now been lost; LA's
impoverished public realm, no
longer serves, in her view,
'adequately to secure, preserve
and enhance our two most
fundamental individual rights,
which are our privacy and our
property. These rights are
guaranteed under the
Constitution as social policy,
but are undermined every day
in physical reality.' Her belief

stems from the initial
connection between public
open space and personal
freedom, going back to the
primary right of assembly, and
national associations with the
village green at Lexington
Massachusetts, where 'the
shot heard round the world'
that began the revolution, was
fired. The Downtown Strategic
Plan which has identified and
pursued a number of 'catalytic'
urban improvement projects in
the area is more than just
another zoning map to this firm,
who have approached it on a
fundamental level, as the
beginning of a return to a sense
of community. In their scheme
for the Metrolink Bus Plaza at
Union Station, Moule &
Polyzoides studied the impact
of new Red Line, Blue Line,
Metrolink, RTV and Dash
services on the locality and
developed a responsive urban
design plan together with
unifying architectural, signage
and lighting proposals.

The Concert Hall provides a fitting, more civic-scaled companion piece to the much-admired Museum of Contemporary Art by Arata Isozaki nearby. Completed in 1986, MOCA displays the formal preoccupations evident in Isozaki's earlier work, in his evolving studies of cubes and vaults in permutations abstracted from, rather than produced by, function. A noticeable difference, however, is that the detachment that characterizes past examples, such as the Gunma or Oita museums, is absent here, in what amounts to a model of civic respectability and contextual good manners, quietly blending into the background. For some time after the building was finished, that background was still a matter of conjecture, as developers manoeuvred to make the most of changing circumstances in a segment of downtown which has now been transformed. Isozaki's restraint was not entirely voluntary, however, and was partially dictated by the economic forces at work in the area. The final result of this complex combination of design sensibilities and commercial imperative, is a remarkably serene and handsome building, sheathed in an elegant palette of materials that add to its quiet sense of dignity and authority. Aside from its role as a catalyst for cultural institutions that have followed, MOCA has also inspired other architects in the city, providing a rich formal vocabulary that may easily be traced through various offices since its completion.

Each of the initiatives discussed above, and many more, have now been incorporated into a co-ordinated overall plan for the area, intended to make Los Angeles into a world-class city. First begun in 1988, at the instigation of the City Hall, under the supervision of a large, citizen-based group called the 'Downtown Strategic Plan Advisory Committee', the plan originally concentrated on the central business district, but was expanded in 1991 to include the eastern portion of downtown. From the beginning, an unshakeable and novel article of faith has been that the physical structure of the downtown area can play a formative part in bringing the heterogeneous cultures of Los Angeles together. Such optimism, however, is certainly at odds with the reality of poverty and crime that now governs in these areas,

and yet a team of consultants from ten urban planning groups, headed by Elizabeth Moule and Stefanos Polyzoides, is undeterred by the obvious disparities that exist, determined to reshape downtown within the fabric of the neighbourhoods around it. Bounded by Elysian and Exposition Parks on the north and south, the palimpsest of the Los Angeles River on the east, and the Wilshire Corridor on the west, the outline plan has been formulated around six general principles. The first of these is the idea of continuity and locality, focusing on existing solutions. As a response to the limited resources now available to carry out large-scale restructuring of the city, the Downtown Strategic Plan has been formulated on the more realistic premise that future urban development must be based on existing conditions, and physical structures now in place. This premise not only makes economic sense, but also reflects a broader, more international view, which recognizes that every great city has an individual character only made possible by accretion over time. As a relatively young city, downtown Los Angeles has just begun that process and can only achieve the 'world class' status it now seeks if it is allowed to continue, without undergoing the major surgery that has been typical of other urban redevelopment projects across the country.

Secondly there is the belief that neighbourhoods and districts are a key to growth. In an initiative of this scope, the eventual responsibility to continue it after physical rebuilding is complete, can only be realized by establishing clear boundaries. The plan approaches the downtown area as a 'mosaic' of neighbourhoods and districts, which will be connected by open space and various kinds of transportation systems. For planning purposes, a neighbourhood has been defined as a primarily residential area with local retail shops, limited by pedestrian access to a central focal point, where offices and institutional buildings may be located.

Thirdly, two zones, 'the City' and 'the Market' have been identified, to help differentiate the pattern of this 'mosaic', which is distinctly different from any other urban centre in Southern California. Moule & Polyzoides have labelled the area around the Civic

Centre, delineated by the residential neighbourhoods west of the Harbour Freeway, north of the Hollywood Freeway and east of Alameda, as 'the City'. It contains mixed, intense concentrations of office, retail, residential entertainment and recreational activities, as well as some of the most identifiably important places in Los Angeles, such as Chinatown, El Pueblo, Little Tokyo, the financial district and the University of Southern California. To distinguish the wholesale and retail areas to the south-east, they have labelled the area connecting directly into South Central Los Angeles as 'the Markets', in recognition of the major industries located there.

Fourthly, the quality of the public realm is an important issue since there is a direct connection between the quality and accessibility of public space and commonly held values. One of the principal, formal ideas of the Downtown Strategic Plan is the expansion of the amount of open space inside its boundaries, mostly from reclaimed areas.[26]

Fifthly, the new train, trolley bus and bus system now being implemented is seen as a great opportunity to counteract the insulating influence that the automobile has had, and the open space around it is described in the plan as 'the primary means of weaving the pedestrian neighbourhoods and districts of downtown together again.'[27]

Sixth and last, the Downtown Strategic Plan has identified 'catalytic projects' which will generate change. These are defined not only by their intrinsic architectural value, but also by 'the physical, economic and social change they effect around them'. Several existing landmarks have been identified as 'catalytic' because they have the capacity to order and direct the future form of the city, and can unify the entire strategic plan.

The 'Silver Book' plan, produced in 1972, has been given high marks for transforming Los Angeles into the financial centre of the West Coast, having been responsible for the fact that the four largest

savings institutions in the United States, and many large international banks, are now located there. The Downtown Strategic Plan which now replaces it has been structured to encourage the physical fabric of the city to grow into its new image. The difference between the two sets of guidelines is indicative of the dramatic change of course that has taken place in the last 20 years, since the 'Silver Book' concentrated on economic growth, and the Downtown Strategic Plan now addresses the social equity issues which are obviously so pressing, by attempting literally to bring the city together. It anticipates no less than 100,000 new residents within the boundaries it has established, as well as 25 million square feet of office space, both largely accommodated through guidelines outlining the restoration and rehabilitation of 300 existing buildings in the area.

If there is any danger in such a comprehensive process, as past examples of such gentrification indicate there usually is, it is that in their zeal for interconnectedness and civic verve, the planners may go too far. Proposals for the revitalization of Broadway, which is now a busy commercial street in the middle of the Downtown area, are a good example of such excess. In seeking to recreate it in the image of its New York namesake, and revealing many civic insecurities in the process, planners have tried to paint a picture of a sanitized commercial street 'enlivened' by the restoration of the old theatres along it; but the concealed agenda has been the eradication of the very diversity they claim to want to create. Broadway, as it exists today, is conclusive proof, if further proof were needed, that Los Angeles really is 'the capital of the Third World', even though the jury is still out on the question of whether or not the United States will eventually join this club.[28] At any given hour between 10 am and midnight, on any day of the week except Sunday, it is crammed with decidedly non-Caucasian shoppers who seem to occupy every inch of space between storefront and

Walt Disney Concert Hall
Downtown Los Angeles,
1988-96
Frank Gehry
Because of its monumentality and rich limestone casing, the Disney Concert Hall represents a departure for Frank Gehry who has previously been known for disjointed, fragmented urban statements. The first contemporary civic parallel that comes to mind is James Stirling's Staatsgalerie in Stuttgart, in which stone cladding is used in an obviously insubstantial way to symbolize the demystification of a hitherto socially exalted urban institution. Gehry lifts the hem of the limestone mantle in certain places around the curvilinear periphery to 'invite the public in,' but the parti, in spite of its swoops and flourishes, is nonetheless traditional.

curb along both sides of the street, in a scene that could just as easily be found in Mexico City or Hong Kong. In the gentrification of downtown which is now underway, however, such scenes are disturbing, in spite of the fact that Broadway is one of the most truly social and lively meeting places in the entire city, because its occupants do not fit the economic profile created for the area.

Such value judgements about what Broadway, or Pershing Square, or Bunker Hill should be, in spite of all the well-meaning gestures towards inclusiveness, raise real questions about which constituency the new Los Angeles is really intended for, and whether or not all of the recent architectural initiatives there are not just a circling of the wagons by a threatened wealthy elite. If displaced again, the thousands of shoppers on Broadway will certainly find somewhere else to go, and probably return to the neighbourhoods that served them before this happy accident was discovered and grew. The re-opening of the theatres there, which will have limited times of operation, may superficially make this street seem like the West Coast version of its nominal counterpart in New York, and return it to a more predictable level of use and user, but the usual degree of sterility that accompanies such cycles will certainly follow as an inevitable corollary of the change. Sanitized, stereotypical ethnicity, of the kind found on Olvera Street, with its movie set quality and mariachi bands, is apparently acceptable, but Broadway is too raw and disturbing, a graphic reminder of the real social equation in the city today and the demographic predictions for the future. Perhaps the sense of pride to which architects such as Ricardo Legoretta refer in describing recent changes like Pershing Square, is restricted to those who will support such projects because they convey the image they expect. Legorreta has lyrically described how important he felt it was that Pershing Square should convey the same feeling as the plazas of his own country because the Latino population of Los Angeles is rising dramatically, and the community should have places to gather. His final scheme, evolved in collaboration with Hanna/Olin, is sensitive and logical as an optimum use of the limited resources available; but the question here, as in many other

instances throughout the city, seems to be one of comparable values and cultural attenuation.

In the Pershing Square scheme, this distance may be seen in the abstract representations of the San Andreas fault and the Pacific Ocean, in the stylized, symmetrical orange groves inscribed on the ground plane of the park, or even Legoretta's tall and elegant sculptural tower, elements which are hardly intended to have widely popular appeal, just as Gehry's aesthetic gesture of 'pulling up the hem' of the Disney Concert Hall, to make it accessible to the people, will really do little to bridge the deep racial and economic divisions which are becoming more evident in Los Angeles with each passing day. But at least attempts to find ways to stitch the city together, either by enlightened developers such as Maguire Thomas and Frederick Smith, or by grassroots organizations such as the Los Angeles Local Initiative Support Corporation, which provides resources for the non profit-making developers operating in inner city neighbourhoods, are now in evidence.

The ecologies of Evil, Neighbourhood and Downtown aside, something has slowly, almost imperceptively, changed in the city. In keeping with the eastern philosophies that are so popular in Los Angeles, those changes continue in positive and negative, delightful and disturbing ways, that seem to be entering a new phase. Against such a background, the trite, popular image of Los Angeles as a city with no centre is beginning to be dispelled, and virtuoso performances by various architects, prompted by reactions to individual perceptions of isolation, are bound to have less meaning. Market forces, and the need to establish a singular identity that they engender, are certain to enable such architects to continue, and they will inevitably attract as much attention as they have in the past. Beneath the stereotypes that such projects serve to perpetuate, however, is an extremely complex phenomenon that is based on more historical precedents than is generally realized. If Los Angeles is to become the prototypical city for the rest of the nation, as so many predict, those who are betting that the prototype will be inclusive, and based on those precedents, seem to stand the best chance of being proven correct.

Notes

Chapter I

Confronting Autopia

1 Joel Garreaux, *The Edge City: Life on the New Frontier* (New York: Doubleday, 1992).

2 Paul Zygas, 'The Eclectic Tradition', *Architectural Design* Profile, 1981, pp. 47-50.

3 Reyner Banham, *Los Angeles: The Architecture of Four Ecologies* (Harmondsworth and New York: Penguin Books, 1971), p. 214.

4 For a general description see David Rieff, *Los Angeles: The Capital of the Third World* (New York: Simon & Schuster, 1991).

5 Walter Burkert, *Homo Necans* (Berkeley: University of California, 1983). See also J.B. Jackson, 'The Timing of Towns', *Architecture California*, vol. 14, no. 2, November 1992, p. 7.

6 Banham, *Los Angeles: The Architecture of Four Ecologies*, *op. cit.*, p. 213.

7 Peter Plagens, 'The Ecology of Evil', *Art Forum*, December 1972, p. 67.

8 Carey McWilliams, *Southern California: An Island on the Land* (Salt Lake City: Peregrine Smith, 1983), p. 6.

Chapter II

Precedents and Continuities: Putting down Roots

1 McWilliams, *Southern California: An Island on the Land*, *op. cit.*, p. 29.

2 *Ibid.*, p. 29.

3 *Ibid.*, p. 30.

4 *Ibid.*, p. 21.

5 David Gebhard and Harriette von Breton, *Architecture in California: 1868-1968* (Santa Barbara: University of California, 1968), p. 16.

6 Sara Holmes Boutelle, *Julia Morgan Architect* (New York: Abbeville Press, 1988), p. 16.

7 *Ibid.*, p. 174.

8 Kathryn Smith, 'Frank Lloyd Wright: Hollyhock House and Olive Hill, 1914-1924', *Journal of the Society of Architectural Historians*, March 1979.

9 Kenneth Frampton, 'The Usonian Legacy', *Architectural Review*, vol. CLXXXII, no. 1090, December 1987, p. 26.

10 *Ibid.*, p. 27.

11 'Frank Lloyd Wright in Los Angeles, 1919-1926:

An Architecture for the Southwest', *Municipal Art Gallery Exhibition Program*, January 1988.

12 *Ibid.*

13 *Ibid.*

14 Mike Davis, 'Back to the Future: Are Bungalows the Answer?' *Los Angeles Times*, 26 April 1992.

15 Robert Gregory Brown, 'The California Bungalow in Los Angeles: A Study in Origins and Classifications', MA thesis, University of California, Los Angeles, 1964, p. 2.

16 *Ibid.*, p. 7.

17 *Ibid.*, p. 16.

18 Edward Bosley, *Gamble House: Greene and Greene* (London: Phaidon Press, 1993), p. 19.

19 *Ibid.*, p. 7.

20 Brown, 'The California Bungalow in Los Angeles', *op. cit.*, p. 41.

21 Kenneth Frampton, 'The Usonian Legacy', *op. cit.*, p. 26.

22 Letter from R.M. Schindler to his parents-in-law, quoted in Kathryn Smith, *R. M. Schindler House, 1921-22* (Los Angeles: Friends of the Schindler House, 1987), p. 18.

23 *Ibid.*, p. 19.

24 For a complete discussion see David Gebhard and Harriette von Breton, *Architecture in California, 1868-1968* (Santa Barbara: University of California, 1968), pp. 18-22.

Chapter III

The Case Study House Programme: 'The Style that Nearly' revisited

1 Kevin Starr, 'The Case Study House Program and the Impending Future: Some Regional Considerations', in *Blue Prints for Modern Living: History and Legacy of the Case Study Houses* (Cambridge, Mass.: MIT Press in conjunction with the Museum of Contemporary Art, Los Angeles, 1989), p. 140.

2 Esther McCoy, 'Arts & Architecture Case Study Houses', in *Blue Prints for Modern Living: History and Legacy of the Case Study Houses*, *op. cit.*, pp. 15-16.

3 *Ibid.*, p. 17.

4 Reyner Banham, 'Klarheit, Ehrlichkeit, Einfachkeit and wit too!: The Case Study Houses in the World's

Eye', in *Blue Prints for Modern Living: History and Legacy of the Case Study Houses, op. cit.*, p. 104.

5   Esther McCoy, *Case Study Houses, 1945-1962*, 2nd edition (Santa Monica: Hennessey & Ingalls, Inc., 1977), p. 57.

6   McCoy, 'Arts & Architecture Case Study Houses', *op. cit.*, p. 53.

7   Amelia Jones and Elizabeth A. T. Smith, 'The 36 Case Study Projects', in *Blue Prints for Modern Living: History and Legacy of the Case Study Houses, op. cit.*, p. 51.

8   McCoy, *Case Study Houses, 1945-1962, op. cit.*

9   Paul Goldberger, 'When Modernism Kissed the Land of Golden Dreams', *New York Times*, 10 December 1989, p. 42.

10   Pierre Koenig, interview with K. Kirkpatrick, 16 October 1992.

11   Elizabeth A. T. Smith, Introduction to *Blue Prints for Modern Living: History and Legacy of the Case Study Houses, op. cit.*, p. 12.

12   *Ibid.*, p. 13.

13   Elizabeth A. T. Smith, 'Extending the Case Study Concept: Newly Commissioned Works', in *Blue Prints for Modern Living: History and Legacy of the Case Study Houses, op. cit.*, p. 213.

14   *Ibid.*, p. 213.

15   *Ibid.*, p. 213.

16   *Ibid.*, p. 213.

17   *Ibid.*, p. 214.

Chapter IV

Frank Gehry: Los Angeles and its Discontents

1   Pritzker Prize Award book, 1989, acceptance speech by Frank O. Gehry, no pagination.

2   'Profiles: A Touch for the Now', *New Yorker Magazine*, 29 July 1991, p. 44.

3   Peter Schjeldahl, 'The Eye of the Revolution', *Art in America*, April 1981, pp. 78-79.

4   Brochure supplied by Gehry office.

5   James Steele, 'LA and the Reinvention of the City', *Architectural Design*, 1991, pp. 36-38.

6   Robert Venturi, Denise Scott Brown and Steven Izenour, *Learning from Las Vegas* (Cambridge, Mass.: MIT Press, 1972).

7   Garreaux, *The Edge City, op. cit.*, p. 15.

8   Pilar Vilades, 'The 1980s', in *The Architecture of Frank Gehry*, (New York: Rizzoli, in conjunction with the Walker Art Center, 1986), p. 158.

9   Philip Johnson, Introduction to *Eric Owen Moss: Buildings and Projects* (New York: Rizzoli, 1991).

10   John Pastier, 'Distillation of a Paradoxical City', *Architecture*, May 1985, p. 202.

11   Gavin Macrae-Gibson, *The Secret Life of Buildings: An American Mythology for Modern Architecture* (Cambridge, Mass. and London: MIT Press, 1985), p. 11.

12   *Ibid.*, p. 13.

13   Fredric Jameson, *Postmodernism or the Cultural Logic of Late Capitalism* (Durham: Duke University Press, 1992), p. 113.

14   *Ibid.*, p. 121.

15   Frank Gehry, project description issued by the Gehry office.

16   Frank Gehry, project description issued by the Gehry office.

17   *Ibid.*

18   *Ibid.*

19   Clement Greenberg, 'Avant Garde and Kitsch', in *Art and Culture* (Boston: Beacon Press, 1961), pp. 3-21.

20   Max Horkheimer and Theodor Adorno, *Dialectic of Enlightenment* (New York: Continuum, 1987), p. 48.

21   *Ibid.*, p. 49.

22   Jean Baudrillard, 'Simulacra and Simulations', *Selected Writings* (Oxford: Polity Press, 1988), p. 166.

23   *Ibid.*, p. 168.

24   Victor Burgin, *The End of Art Theory: Criticism and Postmodernity* (New Jersey: Humanities Press, 1986), p. 40.

25   Madan Sarap, *Post Structuralism and Post Modernism* (Geneva: The University of Geneva Press, 1989), pp. 6-33.

26   Frank Israel, interview with the author, 10 November 1992.

Chapter V

Disregarding Boundaries: The Cult of Individuality

1   Andreas Papadakis et al., *Theory and Experimentation* (London: Academy Editions, 1992), p. 58. 'When one hits the occasional condition such

as a funny old city like Los Angeles — on the
occasions when it did building — you do find that
the guys teaching are the guys doing some hickory-
dickory thing down the same street; and the guys you
see in the morning in class are down there planing
the wood.' (Peter Cook.)

2 Southern California Institute of Architecture,
Academic Catalogue, 1990-91, opening statement by
Michael Rotondi.

3 *SciArc Newsletter*, 30 November 1992, p. 2.

4 Papadakis et al., *Theory and Experimentation*,
op. cit., p. 49.

5 Martin Esslin, *The Theatre of the Absurd*
(Harmondsworth: Penguin Books, 1977), p. 22.

6 *Ibid.*, p. 23.

7 Thom Mayne, interview with the author, 5 December
1992. Reproduced here with the author's gratitude.

8 *Ibid.*

9 Papadakis et al., 'Thomas Mayne', in *Theory and
Experimentation*, *op. cit.*, p. 47.

10 Eric Owen Moss, interview with the author,
7 December 1992.

11 *Eric Owen Moss: Buildings and Projects*,
op. cit., p. 15.

12 *Ibid.*, p. 112.

13 'One more thing. The Yucatán is a productive
reference. It gets you outside the conventional
Western lineage of architectural debate – gets you
outside to go inside.' Eric Owen Moss, 'Small
Immensities', unpublished.

14 Eric Owen Moss, interview with the author,
7 December 1992.

15 *Eric Owen Moss: Buildings and Projects*, *op.
cit.*, p. 15.

16 Papadakis, Broadbent and Toy, *Free Spirit in
Architecture* (London: Academy Editions, 1992),
p. 15.

17 *Ibid.*, p. 243.

18 *Ibid.*, p. 244.

19 Lebbeus Woods, *One Five Four* (New York:
Princeton Architectural Press, 1989).

20 Lebbeus Woods, 'Terra Nova', *Architecture &
Urbanism*, August 1991.

Chapter VI

**Architecture and Community: Divining a Sense
of Place**

1 Frank Israel, interview with the author,
10 November 1992.

2 *Ibid.*

3 *Ibid.*

4 Frank Israel, 'Cities Within', in *The Architecture of
Frank Israel* (New York: Rizzoli, 1992), pp. 13-20.

5 Frank Israel, interview with the author,
10 November 1992.

6 Project description issued by the Israel office.

7 Charles Moore, 'You Have to Pay for the Public Life',
Perspecta 9/10, 1965, p. 58.

8 *Building Types*, courtesy Moule & Polyzoides, 1993.

9 Buzz Yudell, interview with the author,
5 September 1992.

10 *Ibid.*

11 Project description issued by Mark Cigolle and
Katherine Coleman.

Chapter VII

The Search for Civitas and Several New Ecologies

1 Ivan Fallon, 'State of the Union', *The Sunday Times
Magazine*, 6 September 1992, p. 24.

2 *Ibid.*, p. 23.

3 *LA 2000: A City for the Future* (Los Angeles: Los
Angeles 2000 Committee, 1988).

4 Fallon, 'State of the Union', *op. cit.*, p. 25.

5 Jean Baudrillard, *America*, trans. Chris Turner
(London and New York: 1983), p. 16.

6 *Ibid.*, p. 18.

7 *Ibid.*, p. 20.

8 David Reiff, *Los Angeles: Capital of the Third World*
(New York: Simon and Schuster, 1991).

9 Rod Lurie, 'The Big Dis', *Los Angeles Magazine*,
November 1992, p. 122.

10 Plagens, 'The Ecology of Evil', *op. cit.*, p. 72.

11 *Ibid.*, p. 73.

12 *Ibid.*, p. 71.

13 *Ibid.*, p. 69.

14 Katherine Usher Henderson, *Joan Didion*
(New York: Frederick Ungar Publishing, 1981).

15 Joan Didion, *Play it as it Lays* (New York: Bantam
Books, 1970).

16 Mike Davis, 'Freeze Frame LA', symposium at the
Museum of Contemporary Art, Los Angeles,
6 October 1992.

17 *Ibid.*

18 McWilliams, *Southern California: An Island on the
Land*, *op. cit.*, p. 23.

19 *Ibid.*, p. 24.

20 Davis, 'Freeze Frame LA', *op. cit.*

21 Douglas Suisman, *Los Angeles Boulevard* (Los
Angeles Forum for Architecture and Urban Design,
1989), pp. 5-8.

22 Robert Harris, 'A New Framework for Rebuilding in
Downtown LA', *Urban Land*, October 1992, p. 36.

23 Project description issued by the I.M. Pei office.

24 *Ibid.*

25 Leon Whiteson, 'High Note', *Los Angeles Times*,
15 September 1991, p. K-14.

26 Description of the Downtown Strategic Plan issued by
the office of Moule & Polyzoides. Project Team:
Elizabeth Moule & Stefanos Polyzoides, Architects &
Urbanists (Lead Consultant); Duany/Plater-Zyberk,
Architects (Architects & Urban Designers); Peter
deBretteville, Architect; Susan Haviland, Architect;
Hanna/Olin Ltd (Landscape Architect); Telemark
Community Builders (Implementation).

27 *Ibid.*

28 Rieff, *Los Angeles: Capital of the Third World*,
op. cit., 1991.

Select Bibliography

Books

Banham, Reyner. *Los Angeles: The Architecture of Four
Ecologies*. Harmondsworth and New York, 1971.

Baudrillard, Jean. *America*. Trans. Chris Turner.
London and New York, 1988.

——. *Simulations*. New York, 1983.

Betsky, A, J. Chase and L. Whiteson. *Experimental
Architecture in Los Angeles*. Introduction by Frank
Gehry. New York, 1990.

Boutelle, Sara Holmes. *Julia Morgan Architect*. New
York, 1988.

Brodsley, David. *LA Freeway*. Berkeley, 1981.

Brown, Robert Gregory. 'The California Bungalow in
Los Angeles: A Study in Origins and
Classifications'. MA thesis, University of
California, Los Angeles, 1964.

Carr, Harry. *Los Angeles: City of Dreams*. New York,
1935.

Clark, R.J. and Thomas Hines. *Los Angeles Transfer:
Architecture in Southern California*. Los Angeles,
1983.

Cook, Peter and Barbara Goldstein. *Los Angeles
Now*. London, 1985.

Culler, Jonathan D. *On Deconstruction: Theory and
Criticism after Structuralism*. Ithaca, N.Y., 1982.

Davis, Mike. *City of Quartz: Excavating the Future in
Los Angeles*. New York, 1992.

Dickson, Keith A. *Towards Utopia: A Study of
Brecht*. Oxford and New York, 1978.

Didion, Joan. *Play it as it Lays*. New York, 1970.

Downs, Anthony. *Urban Problems and Prospects*.
Chicago, 1970.

Dumke, Glenn S. *The Boom of the Eighties in
Southern California*. San Marino, 1944.

Fenton, Frank. *A Place in the Sun*. New York, 1942.

Fogelson, Robert M. *The Fragmented Metropolis:
Los Angeles, 1850-1930*. Cambridge, Mass., 1967.

Gabler, Neal. *An Empire of Their Own: How the
Jews Invented Hollywood*. New York, 1988.

Garreaux, Joel. *The Edge City: Life on the New
Frontier*. New York, 1992.

Gebhard, David. *LA in the Thirties, 1931-1941*.
Santa Barbara and Salt Lake City, 1975.

——. *Romanza: The California Architecture of Frank
Lloyd Wright*. San Francisco, 1988.

——. *Schindler*. London, 1971.

Gebhard, David and Harriette von Breton.
Architecture in California, 1868-1968. Santa
Barbara, 1968.

Germany, Lisa. *Harwell Hamilton Harris*. Austin,
Texas, 1991.

Glaab, Charles N. and Theodore A. Brown. *The
History of Urban America*. London, 1967.

Gleye, Paul, in collaboration with the Los Angeles
Conservancy, Julius Shulman and Bruce Boehner.
The Architecture of Los Angeles. Los Angeles,
1981.

Goodwin, H. Marshall, Jr. 'California's Growing
Freeway System'. PhD dissertation, University of
California, Los Angeles, 1969.

Greenstein, Paul, Nigey Lennon and Lionel Rolfe.

Bread and Hyacinths: The Rise and Fall of Utopian LA. Los Angeles, 1992.

Halprin, Lawrence. *Freeways*. New York, 1966.

Henderson, Katherine Usher. *Joan Didion*. New York, 1981.

Hilton, George W. and John F. Due. *The Electric Interurbans in America*. Stanford, 1960.

Hines, Thomas S. *Richard Neutra and the Search for Modern Architecture*. New York, 1982.

Horkheimer, Max and Theodor W. Adorno. *Dialectic of Enlightenment*. New York, 1972.

Jones, Mark M. 'Finding a Freeway: Environmental Clues in a Path-Choosing Task'. MA thesis, University of California, Los Angeles, 1971.

Kaplan, Sam Hall. *LA Follies*. Los Angeles, 1989.

——. *LA Lost & Found: An Architectural History of Los Angeles*. New York, 1987.

LA 2000: A City for the Future. Los Angeles 2000 Committee, 1988.

Lurie, Alison. *The Nowhere City*. New York, 1967.

Lynch, Kevin. *Images of the City*. Cambridge, Mass., 1960.

Lyon, James K. *Bertolt Brecht in America*. Princeton, N.J., 1980.

McClenahan, Bessie A. *The Changing Urban Neighborhood: From Neighbor to Nigh-Dweller*. Los Angeles, 1929.

McCoy, Esther. 'Arts and Architecture Case Study Houses', in *Blue Prints for Modern Living: History and Legacy of the Case Study Houses*. Cambridge, Mass., 1989, pp. 15-39.

——. *Case Study Houses, 1945-1962*. 2nd ed., Los Angeles, 1977.

——. *Five California Architects*. New York, 1960.

——. *Richard Neutra*. London, 1960.

——. *Vienna to Los Angeles: Two Journeys – Letters between R.M. Schindler and Richard Neutra*. Santa Monica, 1979.

McDaniel, W.A. 'Re-evaluating Freeway Performance in Los Angeles.' MA thesis, University of California, Los Angeles, 1971.

McWilliams, Carey. *Southern California: An Island on the Land*. Santa Barbara and Salt Lake City, 1973.

Marx, Leo. *The Machine in the Garden*.

New York, 1964.

Moore, Charles, Peter Becker and Regula Campbell. *The City Observed: Los Angeles*. New York, 1984.

Neutra, Dione. *Richard Neutra: Promise and Fulfillment 1919-1932*. Carbondale and Edwardsville, 1986.

Rand, Christopher. *Los Angeles: The Ultimate City*. New York, 1967.

Rieff, David. *Los Angeles: Capital of the Third World*. New York, 1991.

Schmidt-Brummer, Horst. *Venice, California: An Urban Fantasy*. New York, 1972.

Scott, Mel. *American City Planning since 1870*. Berkeley, Los Angeles and London, 1971.

Searing, Helen. 'Case Study Houses in the Grand Modern Tradition', in *Blue Prints for Modern Living: History and Legacy of the Case Study Houses*. Cambridge, Mass., 1989, pp. 106-129.

Wallis, Brian, ed. *Art after Modernism: Rethinking Representation*. New York, 1984.

Warner, Sam Bass, Jr. *The Urban Wilderness: A History of the American City*. New York, 1972.

West, Nathanael. *The Day of the Locust*. Alexandria, Va., 1939.

Wright, Frank Lloyd. *An Autobiography*. New York, 1977.

Periodicals

Betsky, Aaron. 'Architecture against Reality: Blueprints of a Nostalgic Future'. *LA Weekly*, 8-14 December 1989, pp. 45-48.

Ericksen, E. Gordon. 'The Superhighway and City Planning: Some Ecology Considerations with Reference to Los Angeles'. *Social Forces*, 28 May 1950, pp. 429-434.

'Freeway Blues: The Dream LA Broke Down'. *Los Angeles Times*, 4 September 1971, I, p. 1.

Goldberger, Paul 'When Modernism Kissed the Land of Golden Dreams'. *New York Times*, 10 December 1989, pp. 42-47.

Goldstein, Barbara. 'The History and Legacy of the Case Study Houses'. *Architecture*, December 1989, p. 19.

Herbert, Ray. 'LA Area Freeways Displace 3,000 a Year'. *Los Angeles Times*, 28 June 1973, II, p. 1.

Hoover, Eleanor. 'Freeway Mystique: More Than "Getting There"'. *Los Angeles Times*, 11 May 1975, II, p. 1.

Kappe, Shelly. 'Idiom of the Fifties: What Really Happened in Los Angeles'. *Architecture California*, 8, no. 6, November/December 1986, pp. 15-25.

Knight, C. 'Exploring Domiciles in Blueprints'. *LA Herald Examiner*, 22 October 1989, E2.

Link, Tony. 'Home Is Where the Art Is'. *LA Life*, 16 October 1989, p. 5.

McCoy, Esther. 'Arts & Architecture Case Study Houses'. *Perspecta 15*, 1975, pp. 55-69.

——. 'LA Case Study Houses: When Shelter was an Art Form'. *LA Times*, 8 October 1989, Editorial/Opinion page.

——. 'Pierre Koenig'. *Zodiac 5*, 1959, pp. 156-166.

'MOCA's Case Study Houses Exhibit and Related Events'. *Journal of the Society of Architectural Historians*, Philadelphia, October/November 1989, pp. 10-12.

Moreland, Graeme. 'Movement Systems'. *Architectural Design* Profile, 1981.

'Museum Exhibit Focuses on Case Study Home Era'. *Los Angeles Times*, 15 October 1989.

Nelson, Howard J. 'The Spread of an Artificial Landscape over Southern California'. *Man, Time, and Space in Southern California*, ed. William L. Thomas, Jr. Special supplement to *Annuals of the Association of American Geographers*, vol. 49, September 1959, pp. 80-100.

Pegrum, Dudley. 'Urban Transport and the Location of Industry in Metropolitan Los Angeles' *Occasional Paper no.2*, Bureau of Business and Economic Research, University of California, Los Angeles, 1963.

Plagens, Peter. 'The Ecology of Evil'. *Art Forum*, December 1972, p. 67.

Walker, Derek (ed.). 'Los Angeles'. *Architectural Design* Profile, 1981.

Woods, Lebbeus. *One Five Four*. Princeton, N.J. 1989.

Zygas, Paul. 'The Eclectic Tradition'. *Architectural Design* Profile, 1981, pp. 47-50.

Index

Photographic Acknowledgements

The publishers and author are grateful to the following for providing illustrations for this book.

The Architectural Collective: 191

Peter Aprahamian: 58t, 58b

Richard Barnes: 20-21, 22, 23, 102, 104, 105, 107

Tom Bonner: 2, 14, 101t, 112tl, 116tl&tr, 120, 121t&b, 122, 124, 125tl, 128-129, 134r, 135b, 136t&b, 144-145, 148-149, 150t, 162-163, 164t, 165

Wayne Cable / Cable Studios: 192

Central Office of Architecture: 150b

Cigolle & Coleman: 19t, 188tr, 189

Peter Cook: 49, 82-83, 84, 85, 126, 130, 133, 138-139, 140, 141, 194, 208, 209, 210, 212-213, 214

Frank Dimster: 188tl

Frank Gehry: 73, 80tl, 81, 90b, 93l&r, 101b, 219

Hodgetts & Fung: 142, 146b&tr, 147

Timothy Hursley: 167, 168, 170-171, 172, 173, 174, 176, 177t, 178-179, 181, 182t, 182b

Arata Isozaki: 211, 215t&b

Frank Israel: 153, 157, 158b, 159l&r, 161r, 164b

Jerde Partnership: 90t

Panos Koulermos: 190t

Charles Lagreco / Architectural Collective: 190b

Lubowicki Lanier: 146tl

Frank Garnier / Hanna/Olin: 206, 207

Moore Ruble Yudell: 166, 169, 175, 177b, 183, 184

Michael Moran: 86-87, 89, 94-95, 98-99, 100, 198-199, 200, 203

Morphosis: 103, 106, 110tl, 111, 112tr, 115, 116b, 117

Eric Owen Moss: 71, 119r&l, 123, 125tr&b, 127, 131, 132, 134l, 135t&c, 137

Marvin Rand: 70r

Sue Mossman: 41t

Moule & Polyzoides: 185t&b, 186, 187, 205, 216tr&b, 218

Grant Mudford: 11, 91, 92, 114, 143t&b, 152, 154, 155, 156, 158t, 160, 161l

John Mutlow Architects: 193

Pei Cobb Freed & Partners: 201l&r

Ralph Rapson: 57

Adèle Naudé Santos: 70l

Julius Shulman: 16, 31, 32-33, 54, 56, 60, 61, 62, 63

Stedelijk Museum, Amsterdam: 74tl

Tim Street-Porter: 6-7, 8-9, 10, 12, 13, 15, 18, 19b, 24, 26-27, 28, 30, 34, 35, 36-37, 38, 39, 40, 42, 44, 45, 46-47, 48, 50, 51, 52, 53, 64, 65, 66-67, 68, 69, 72, 74b, 75, 78, 79, 80t, 80b, 88, 96, 97, 108-109, 110r, 113, 118, 196, 197, 202, 204, 216tl

John Uniach: 221

Douglas White: 151